Aleister Crowley in full masonic regalia

Blood on the Altar
The Secret History of the World's Most Dangerous Secret Society

CRAIG HEIMBICHNER

Independent History and Research
Coeur d'Alene • Idaho

First Edition
January, 2005
ISBN: 0-9703784-3-2

Printed in the U.S.A.

Independent History & Research
PO Box 849 Coeur d'Alene, Idaho 83816

www.revisionisthistory.org

CONTENTS

Preface

"Whosoever disregards this does so at his own risk and
peril."
Book of the Law [1]

Today increasing attention is being given to the role of
secret societies in world affairs, due in part to the
"coincidence" of the United States presidential race of
2004, in which both candidates, Republican George W.
Bush and Democrat John F. Kerry, publicly admitted
membership in the same secret society, known as the
Order of Skull and Bones. This necromantic Order
received temporary prominence in 2004 as part of the
ongoing orchestration of covert control of the masses. As
journalists David Wise and Thomas B. Ross wrote in their
landmark exposé of U.S. intelligence, *The Invisible
Government:*
"There are two governments in the United States today.
One is visible. The other is invisible. The first is the
government that citizens read about in their newspapers
and children study about in their civics books. The second
is the interlocking, hidden machinery....The Invisible
Government is not a formal body. It is a loose, amorphous
grouping of individuals and agencies..." [2]
The control of the masses indeed possesses an exoteric
level, the illusion of which is taught in civics classes and
played out before us in the media in the form of elections,
campaigns and public laws. The far more important side of
government, however, is the esoteric, which at the highest
level involves a manipulation of the mass consciousness
with a watchful eye, by a network of psychological power
brokers, the "Invisible Government of Wise and Ross,"
later described by Walter Bowart in his 1978 classic,

---

[1] All quotes in chapter headings are from Aleister Crowley's
Book of the Law, the canonical text of the OTO (York Beach,
Maine: Weiser Books, 1976 reprint of the 1938 edition).

[2] David Wise and Thomas B. Ross, *The Invisible Government*
(New York: Random House, 1964).

Operation Mind Control, as the "Cryptocracy." The Cryptocracy is not a myth, it seeks to transform humanity through an alchemical processing of the mass consciousness or Group Mind which involves various tests and corresponding responses through channels linked to secret societies. The result is both psychological and cultural control; but more importantly, *transformation.* The Cryptocracy has essentially kept the mind of the masses cooking in a cauldron like a Renaissance alchemist, and occasionally tastes, adds ingredients, and stirs.

Yet while the Order of Skull and Bones is currently driving the busload of squabbling, dumbed-down "Goyim," another secret society is processing them, as it processed the 60s generation, and the elite intellectuals since the early years of the 20th century -- in the alchemist's beaker known as education. Modern education possesses a formal side, as exhibited in the public schools, and an extremely important informal side which includes the all-important amorphous "school" called pop culture, whose school desks are sofas situated in front of plasma television screens and whose guest lecturers are DVDs, or — at least at one time — science fiction novels. The secret society to which I am referring heavily impacted both Sci-Fi and Hollywood, helping to sow seeds of transformation in the mass psyche.

In addition, this Order maintained its status and membership and even worked depraved rituals among military and intelligence channels, all the while possessing important ties to the heart of the space program. This multifaceted but powerful cult numbered among its leaders the British Intelligence Officer Aleister Crowley (1875-1947), the self-styled "Great Beast 666." It was Crowley, dubbed "The Wickedest Man in the World" by the English paper *John Bull,* who gave this secret society its most potent modern shape and direction, effectively recreating it in his own bestial image. It has since adapted and grown, taking an increasingly decentralized and laid-back outer form, while remaining indelibly stamped with the legacy of the Beast.

The organization to which I am referring is known by many names, in Latin it is called the *Ordo Templi Orientis*; in German, the *Orientalischer Templer-Orden* and in English, the "Order of Oriental Templars." But its most widely recognized appellation is simply the "OTO."

The OTO currently has lodges and "power zones" across the world, including Israel, Russia and South America, and still claims to be the "graduate school" for the old prototypical fraternal order and "service club" known as the Freemasons. Many Freemasons would dispute this claim, but we will see that such protests reflect either ignorance or an attempt at deception of the "Cowans" (outsiders), including deception of lower-level dupes within their own system of lodges. The OTO is a traditional "fringe Masonic" or "irregular" Order, a special group structure which exists in a fraternal relationship with top members of Grand Lodge "regular" Freemasonry, minus official sanction, enabling convenient public disavowals and denial by the Grand Lodge when incriminating activities of these "irregular" lodges occasionally reach public awareness. In the case of the *"Propaganda Due"* or "P2" scandal in Italy in 1981, which involved blackmail, murder, the Government of Italy and the Vatican Bank, the P2 lodge was hastily dubbed "irregular" by Freemasonry, although the $26.4 million dollars involved in the criminal enterprise were certainly regular enough. [3]

As one example, the following statement comes from an OTO source who, at the conclusion, reveals his relationship with the Grand Lodge. While it contains a few ambiguities, it highlights the often-denied relationship between the OTO and "regular" Freemasonry:

"Freemasons claim that they arose out of the masonic (i.e. those who build with stone) guilds of the middle ages, and intimate that their actual origins stem from the Knights Templar. By the time they fully revealed themselves to the public (at the formation of the United Grand Lodge of England in 1717), they claimed that they had evolved from 'operative' masons (actual builders/architects), into 'speculative' masons (pondering the philosophical morality in the symbols of the builders' craft), who derived elaborate ceremonies and morality

---

[3] For the story of the P2 Lodge, cf. Stephen Knight, *The Brotherhood: The Secret World of The Freemasons.*

plays in order to explicate and get the point across, with liberal subliminal doses of qabalistic symbolism. The way I see it, the evolution of the masons was from operative to speculative, but I would say that it was in a Rosicrucian sense rather than a masonic sense. I see in the rituals of Freemasonry an attempt to infuse classical Rosicrucian symbolism into masonic initiation in such a manner as would not be inflammatory to such that would find it objectionable. The rituals of OTO go a step toward tearing down the veil concealing that additional symbolism...reformulated as a sort of 'new aeon' freemasonry. However, OTO makes no claim to make 'masons,' but rather 'magicians,' as a comparison of degree titles between the two systems would suggest. Similarly, the A.'.A.'. is a reformulation of the traditional Rosicrucian model (i.e. Golden Dawn, AMORC etc.) with a new aeon spin... [4]

The Essence of Freemasonry

Although it is beyond the scope of this book to give a foundational history of Freemasonry, the essence of Freemasonry can be traced to the current of ancient Sumerian worship of "Shaitan" (Satan). This current was given shape in ancient Egypt and Babylon, but ironically was most effectively preserved from disintegration through the oral teaching of its rabbinical heirs in the form of the "traditions of the ancients" or "elders."

In the Old Testament, the Israelites were drawn repeatedly to the "ways of Egypt," the most striking symbolical moment being the worship of the Golden Calf (Exodus 32:1-35). The Egyptian-inspired rabbinic oral teaching was later opposed by Jesus Christ, but nonetheless survived the destruction of the Second Temple in 70 A.D., after which it was gradually committed to writing by rabbis and became known as the Babylonian Talmud and the Kabbalah. The tyrannical discipline of the pagan priesthood of Egypt and Babylon was veiled in the Talmud beneath references to the Scriptures of the

---

[4] Information from a past Master of both a Masonic Lodge and an OTO "Oasis."

Israelites; similarly, the Kabbalah preserved an occult teaching within an occasional appearance of piety, orthodoxy, and commentaries on the Mosaic texts of the Pentateuch. This formalized religion of bureaucratic oppression (Talmud) and pagan gnosis (Kabbalah) became known after 70 A.D. as Judaism, utterly distinct from the "Old Testament only" form of religion that was practiced in the centuries after Christ by the tiny minority of Judaic Karaites who suffered violent persecution at the hands of the rabbis, even having their tongues cut out or being flogged to death in Castile, Spain from the 11th century forward, for refusing to acknowledge the authority of the rabbis in Judaism's own version of the inquisition (neatly consigned to historical oblivion).

The rabbinically reworked gnosis survived Apostolic opposition and the denunciations of early Church fathers, by sowing confusion within Christendom, where it was often mistaken for the *sola Scriptura* creed of the ancient Israelites, rather than what it was, a sect top-heavy with unscriptural, man-made tradition and pagan superstition. The Egyptian legacy of Osiris, Isis and Horus, of Set-An and Shaitan, thus survived, preserved in Judaism as though in a petrie dish. As this strange infection was transmitted through generation after generation, it sought new carriers and attempted to spread through covers and fronts. The occult current mutated into various forms, from the Manicheans and Carpocratians to the Cathars and Bogomils. A virulent strain appeared when the Knights Templars were corrupted and transformed into an occult Order. The Order was crushed by Altar and Throne and driven again underground.

A solid occult beachhead was established in England under Elizabeth I, culminating in the Rosicrucian movement, the Renaissance exaltation of magic and alchemy by Heinrich Cornelius Agrippa (1486-1535) and Paracelsus (1493-1541), and later the formation of a socially accepted system of lodges, free to recruit respectable men. This English lodge system, exoterically a brotherhood and fraternal order copied from the Catholic guild of stonemasons, used the symbols of stonemasonry to teach apparently moral lessons, but actually imported kabbalistic symbols from Judaism and reserved its occult teachings for higher initiates. Hence, the new Masonic Lodge became the powerful inner occult channel between countries as it spread across Europe and to America. Thus was born Freemasonry.

Initiates

Publicly professing to worship a vague being called the "Great Architect Of The Universe" (G.A.O.T.U.), the "Blue Lodge" initiates Freemasons through a three-degree ritual system, while other rites, such as the York and Scottish, take an aspiring Mason up through higher degrees, some of which increasingly drop hints regarding the esteem in which a true initiate should hold both occultism and Lucifer, the philosopher's "Light Bearer." [5]

Masons recognize each other by code phrases ("Are you on the level?") and by secret handshakes and gestures; in Western culture they form the original "good-old-boy" system which still rescues members and smashes opponents, originally by murder but today more often by career termination, financial and social ostracism, judicial corruption and scandalous set-ups. Like Al Capone with his Chicago soup kitchens, the Masons cover themselves with many charitable activities, usually performed by one of the "Porch Brethren" (useful idiot). The Freemasons are the prototype of the service clubs that followed Masonry, such as the Rotary. The "Bar Association," the U.S. court and police systems, the Federal government, and military and space program are heavily infiltrated with Freemasons. The Supreme Court and Congress have had key members drawn from the powerful high degree Scottish Rite; several U.S. Presidents have been members of the Lodge, while others have been functioning front men for their power network.

The average "Knife and Fork" Freemason is a pitiable dupe. He gullibly trades his good name to the lodge as a member, in exchange for a mess of pottage in the form of a greased career track. This ignorance can even apply to

---

[5] In the third degree initiation ceremony, the blindfolded candidate is disoriented by a blow to the forehead with a mallet: hence the common expression, "they gave him the Third Degree" used to designate psychological pressure and

upper degrees, which do not automatically guarantee that an individual is among the knowledgeable inner circle. Yet no one can progress through the higher degrees with one eye open and not notice that an occult or esoteric level is being promoted. But where is it?

Enter the OTO

The OTO does not merely hint of occultism, but plunges headlong into the very subjects the high degree Masons are told are reserved to the core of initiation. And at the core of these secrets is the embrace of contradiction, of the "elixir of life," and of the power of blood. Readers can judge for themselves how much of this gnosis is horrifying or simply sickening, the dark doings of the depraved. Readers will risk an encounter with material which scalds innocence and do so at your own peril. Each must decide if this book is a key to needed understanding or merely an unnecessary fascination. It should not be read for the latter reason, for fascination has been too long exploited by the Cryptocracy to turn us from reality and from the proper subjects of awe which greet us each moment in God's creation. Fascination should be restored to embrace the "sacrament of the present moment," as Jean-Pierre de Caussade phrased the delight and holiness of the ongoing activity of the Creator. Easily offended readers should find other reading.

Degenerate kabbalistic secrets form the gnosis of the Cult of the Great Beast Aleister Crowley, truly the grandfather of modern Satanism. These secrets may even have formed the basis of the cult led by Charles Manson, who is alleged to have been affiliated with a renegade "Solar Lodge," formerly of the OTO. These secrets also formed the basis of our space program as propelled by OTO leader John Whiteside Parsons, founder of the Aerojet Corporation and co-founder of NASA's Jet Propulsion Laboratory in Pasadena, California.

This gnosis has shaped Hollywood and American politics and revamped both the Catholic Church and modern culture itself, sparking the spread of Wicca and the modern homosexual movement, ultimately ushering the modern world into what initiates call the era of "Horus the Child," processing our culture, transforming its vestiges of

Christianity into deepening layers of Crowleyanity.

2004 was the centenary of this New Aeon, and the OTO produced a corresponding edition of its main "holy book," a book we shall encounter shortly. The Beast is alive and well in the 21st century, "farming" the goyim as Charles Fort would say, to the point where a set-up like Bonesman A (Bush) versus Bonesman B (Kerry) didn't cause a nanosecond of concern to the average ESPN and porn-addicted couch potato. But the OTO is not finished, as we shall demonstrate, once we understand its origin, purposes, goals, and, in particular, its masters.

I

Beast Cult 101

"...in these are mysteries that no Beast shall divine."

The Cult of the Beast is no trivial affair: it is a powerful, worldwide organization, approximately a century old, with multifarious branches. This occult order arose out of the ashes of the Bavarian Illuminati and condensed within itself all the degrees of Freemasonry, up to and including the almost unheard-of 97th Degree. It is the distillation, the essence, of the most secret of all the secret societies.

A peculiar name for a Beast-Cult, "Order of Oriental Templars," the "OTO." This is intentional. These three letters contain a hint of the advanced-degree's central secret, borrowed from the *Zohar*. [1]

Obscure, but encircling the globe; obscure, but peopled by some of the world's most highly educated men and women; obscure, but working secretly toward the alchemical processing of humanity. Why hasn't the average person heard of it? The OTO does not hide itself completely. On the other hand, it does not advertise itself widely either. [2] Its lodges are not imposing edifices, like a Scottish Rite temple, replete with pagan symbols. One might walk past an OTO lodge and never know it. But for those who seek for it, the OTO will make itself available.

The OTO does not control the whole world, but some of the most monumental historical events in the twentieth century have been "shaped" by the OTO. The OTO works silently, like an invading cancer, an odorless and colorless

---

[1] "Book of Radiance," the primary text of the Kabbalists, studied by advanced students of Judaism.

[2] In the Internet age, "OTO" websites are prolific. But these are mostly touchy-feely public relations ventures and some are even operated by persons who are not initiates. With a few notable exceptions, websites featuring "OTO" and "Do what thou wilt shall be the whole of the law" are a dime-a-dozen, and often serve to confuse rather than inform.

gas. Like a nightmarish Goat of Mendes stealing into a bedroom on a moonlit night, the OTO has crept into many startling places, and literally and figuratively climbed in bed like a corrupt politician.

The cult of the OTO is the essence, the innermost circle, of esoteric Freemasonry (although this fact will be denied by virtually every masonic Lodge). But not only is the historical case for the genuineness of this claim too strong to ignore, inner circle members know the facts of overlapping masonic/OTO memberships, and keep these secrets to themselves.

One might first make contact with the OTO via an erotic poetry reading in which one's reactions are observed and gauged to see if further information should be shared. One might overhear in a coffee shop the greeting of one member to another: "Do what thou wilt shall be the whole of the Law."

If one were allowed to peer inside an OTO lodge in Japan, Brazil, Israel or Texas, one might even see rituals performed by those possessing dual initiation in the related Order of the Beast known as the "Silver Star." Here one would observe a robed initiate perform the Greater Ritual of the Hexagram, [3] a ritual most Masons have never seen, in spite of the clear hints and references to the Kabbalah in the writings of their own leaders, writings the average Mason never studies. [4]

Brilliant and dedicated Freemasons, however, will end up in the OTO. There is really nowhere else for them to go, other than to the Order of the Silver Star, which usually presupposes OTO membership. or, if they are too squeamish, to the more conventional (albeit Luciferian) Hermetic Order of the Golden Dawn.

---

[3] The hexagram or so-called "Star of David," has nothing to do with ancient Israel, King David or the Old Testament.

[4] Commonly spelled Qabalah within the OTO, with emphasis on "magickal" practice and Goddess worship. Spelled Cabala (Latinized), when denoting any group of conspirators; and in rabbinic circles, rendered "Kabbalah" to denominate the original, classic rabbinic teachings of Isaac Luria and other Judaic "sages." See glossary for additional information.

Basic Facts Concerning the OTO

1. Charles Manson, was allegedly affiliated with a southern California group called the "Solar Lodge," said by some to have once had a connection to the OTO. The OTO disavows the connection and the "Solar Lodge" is generally regarded to have been a renegade outfit. The Solar Lodge expounded an End-of the-World outlook, white separatism and sadomasochism. It has been further alleged by certain writers that the Solar Lodge involved drug dealing, blood drinking, child molestation and murder, partly as a means for the psychological programing and conditioning of its members. L. Ron Hubbard, the founder of "Scientology," picked up his Scientology *schtick* while a member of a California OTO unit.

2. The OTO is related to the Palladium rite, Freemasonry's inner sanctum.

3. The OTO includes a worldwide ecclesiastical wing, the "Gnostic Catholic Church." The central liturgy of the OTO is the Gnostic Mass, composed by Aleister Crowley. This rite is celebrated around the world at nightfall every Sunday, by a Priestess enthroned upon an altar while naked (if Crowley's rubrics are followed faithfully). This is not quite a "Black Mass," but has been styled "Gray." [5]

4. Some OTO members have promoted "man/boy love." The immensely influential "sexologist" Alfred Kinsey (1894-1956), author of *Sexual Behavior in the Human Male,* which became the basis of modern sex education, seriously eroding America's traditional morality, was a pederast who used hundreds of children in sex acts connected with his famed "medical research." [6] Kinsey

---

[5] The Gnostic Mass is not a "Black Mass" in the Satanic sense, in which the rubrics of the Roman Catholic Mass are reversed. Rather, the Gnostic Mass conceals its invocations of Satan under names which an initiate only later discovers are synonymous with Satan. In this sense some have styled the OTO rite a "Gray Mass" due to its deceptive, rather than overtly diabolical nature.

[6] Cf. Judith Reisman, *Kinsey: Crimes & Consequences.* Kinsey "included observational reports on the speed of reaching orgasm in 1,888 boys, aged 5 months to adolescence who were timed with a stopwatch" and "147 preadolescent" girls.

cited Crowley as a major inspiration, and was a guest at Crowley's Abbey of Thelema. Kinsey was glorified in a 2004 Hollywood movie from Rupert Murdoch's Fox studio.

5. The OTO has successfully inveigled itself into the Roman Catholic Church, a traditional enemy it despises for its preservation of the message of the crucified Christ, whose image is trampled underfoot in the fifth degree rite of the OTO ritual of the "Sovereign Prince of the Rose-Croix." The OTO fosters an alchemically double-minded blend of awe for traditional Catholic ritual, and antagonism toward Rome; while keeping highly interested in the direction of the Catholic Church and seeking to influence that direction whenever possible.

6. Following the death of the staunchly anti-Masonic Pope Leo XIII in 1903, the OTO nearly gained a Pope from its own ranks, with the narrowly-vetoed papal election of Cardinal Mariano Rampolla del Tindaro (1843-1913), Vatican Secretary of State and secret member of the Masonic Academy. The veto was secured by an alert Catholic expert on occult conspiracy, Monsignor Ernest Jouin of France, who convinced Austrian Emperor Franz-Josef, aided by Cardinal Jan Puzyna, Bishop of Cracow, who invoked an ancient law canceling the election of Cardinal Rampolla.

7. The OTO helped spawn popular enthusiasm among the young for Wicca or "white witchcraft," appropriating much of the energy and direction of the New Age movement and paving the way for the acceptance of the notion of the "good witch" as expressed in the best-selling *Harry Potter* novels.

8. The head of the OTO, British Intelligence Officer Aleister Crowley, and his Judaic secretary, Israel Regudy (a.k.a. "Regardie") are primarily responsible for pioneering obsession with the Kabbalah, from which the contemporary explosion in interest in the Kabbalah among celebrities like Madonna and Britney Spears, is derived.

9. In spite of the utter depravity of the OTO and its occult mission, which strikes objective observers as insane, there is method in the OTO's madness: it has been linked to the highest levels of the governments of the West. Major-General John Frederick Charles Fuller (1878-1966), one of the top military strategists in the history of the

modern era, was Aleister Crowley's right hand man.

In the U.S., the Jet Propulsion Laboratory's chief rocket scientist in Pasadena, California, John Whiteside Parsons, was for several years the leader of the California OTO. Parsons helped to lay the groundwork for the space program and the flights to the moon as "an act of ritual magic." OTO sex and death rituals are performed across the United States, including crazed *magica sexualis* ceremonies involving -- according to the late James Shelby Downard -- Secret Service and FBI personnel at the Mount Palomar Observatory, who performed sex rites with Mr. Downard's estranged wife, Anne, while immersed in light from the star Sirius in the constellation *Canis Major*, beamed through the 200-inch Palomar telescope. (Sirius was the supreme object of veneration in the state religion of ancient Egypt).

10. As a result of its enormous influence on the elite, the OTO has inaugurated and cemented the transformation of the masses -- working in Hollywood, the corporate business world and within the US government -- spreading the "energy of Satan" across the planet, in the words of "Frater Aussik 400," (Kenneth Grant), outer head of the *Ordo Templi Orientis*. [7]

In the eyes of the OTO, the god Horus is upon us, i.e their demonic madness is now our culture's accepted norm; their initiates are now our leaders.

---

[7]

Cf. Kenneth Grant, *The Magical Revival*, and *Aleister Crowley and the Hidden God*.

II

The Blood Brotherhood
of Baphomet

"...let blood flow to my name."

The first contradiction of both the OTO and our culture is an apparent affirmation of life melded with a deep fascination with blood. In its official material, the OTO explains and demands blood sacrifice over and over. In its main "scripture" *The Book of the Law* it is written, "Worship me with fire and blood...let blood flow to my name...Sacrifice cattle, little and big: after a child...Kill and torture; spare not; be upon them!...The best blood is of the moon, monthly: then the fresh blood of a child...then of enemies...This burn: of this make cakes & eat unto me...Also these shall breed lust & power of lust in you at the eating thereof."

The magnum opus of Aleister Crowley and consequently of the OTO, is the weighty tome *Magick*, currently sold in mainstream bookstore chains. In this family-Bible-sized work, the chapter titled "Of the Bloody Sacrifice, and of Matters Cognate," states that, "The animal should therefore be killed within the Circle, or the Triangle, as the case may be, so that its energy cannot escape...For the highest spiritual working one must accordingly choose that victim which contains the greatest and purest force. A male child of perfect innocence and high intelligence is the most satisfactory and suitable victim...The method of killing, however, is practically uniform—the animal should be stabbed to the heart, or its throat severed, in either case by the knife. All other methods of killing are less efficacious; even in the case of crucifixion death is given by stabbing."

This reference to blood sacrifice is far from the only one in the writings of OTO leader Crowley. In the secret instructions given to an initiate of the Eighth Degree, the candidate is given a treatise entitled *Of the Rites of Blood* in which he encounters this statement:

"It is said that there is a sect of the Jewish Brethren called Chassidim whose practice is the sacrifice of man. Thus preferably a child, but also an adult, is taken from among the Gentiles, and ceremonially slain so that not a drop of blood is lost, lest the spirit of the victim, taking refuge in that drop, escape the Exorcist. This blood is then consumed as a sacrament, or employed for talismanic purposes. For once the spirit of the slain one is sealed up into the spilt and gathered blood, it is multiplied in every part thereof, even as in the Mass the Body of Christ is said to be equally in all the myriad consecrated hosts, and His Blood in every drop of consecrated wine, everywhere and for all efficacious."

Crowley has come in for some severe condemnation on account of repeating what is now frequently denounced as a "blood libel" against orthodox rabbis, but Crowley meant no libel: He had inside information, possibly from Sir Richard Francis Burton, that a sect of Judaics did indeed engage in human sacrifice. In his introduction to *Sepher Sephiroth*,a Kabbalistic dictionary which Crowley published in his occult journal *The Equinox*, he writes: "Human sacrifices are today still practiced by the Jews of Eastern Europe, as is set forth at length by the last Sir Richard Burton in the MS. Which the wealthy Jews of England have compassed heaven and earth to suppress..."

Philosopher of Ritual Murder

There is no doubt that Crowley believed in the efficacy of actual blood sacrifice; the passages are too numerous to deny. In Crowley's *The Vision and the Voice* [1] one can read this original footnote, which involves a "blind" or hoodwink:

"The 'Bloody Sacrifice' is commonly regarded as 'Black Magic." But this depends upon the Formula used by the Magician. All taking of life could be reprehensible, even though necessary, were it not for the Formula of Evolution. One should assume into one's own Being, ceremonially, the whole karma of the creature slain; thus building it up into a higher organic structure, and thus

---

[1] Aleister Crowley et al., *The Vision and the Voice* (York Beach, Maine: Samuel Weiser, 1998).

helping it to fulfill its True Will of Aspiration to a higher Form of Life. This is, of course, a gross and material method of working; but it is the only method available in such cases. The animal is in any case doomed to death..."

In the same volume one can find these words: "The supreme Rite would be to bring about a climax in the death of the victim. By this Rite one would attain the summit of Magical Art. Even better would be to slay a girl, preferably a willing victim. After violating her, she should be cut into nine pieces. These should not be eaten, but divided as follows:—head, arms, legs, and quadrisected trunk. The names of the gods appropriate are to be written on the skin, the arms are then to be flayed, and burnt...This Rite should not be employed on ordinary occasions, but rarely, and then for great purposes; it should not be disclosed to any man."

Or consider this passage from other Aleister Crowley official material: "Then again the master shall speak as he will soft words, and with music and what else he will bring forward the Victim. Also he shall slay a young child upon the altar, and the blood shall cover the altar with perfume as of roses."

The OTO denies that any of these passages refer to murder or human sacrifice. The OTO is not entirely disingenuous in hinting that the meaning relates to the physiology of female menstruation. The secrets of the upper degrees of the OTO do indeed involve the employment of a "Scarlet Woman" whose *Elixir Rubeus* is considered the effluvium of *Babalon* (OTO parlance for the Biblical "whore of Babylon"), forming an important emission for the initiate who consumes this mixture as a "sacrament."

One standard OTO ritual involves the crucifixion of a toad after baptizing it as Jesus: "Lo, Jesus of Nazareth, how thou art taken in my snare...as I blot thee out from this earth, so surely shall the eclipse pass...I...therefore condemn thee Jesus the Slave-God, to be mocked and spat upon and scourged and then crucified." Torture of the frog follows, culminating in its stabbing.

It is clear that one can hardly dismiss all of the references in the literature of Crowleyanity to blood sacrifice as figurative. Crowley sacrificed a male goat while it copulated with his consort, Leah Hirsig. Crowley slit its throat, and Hirsig's back was splattered with its blood. One gets closer to the truth by realizing that the communion served in the Gnostic Mass each Sunday night is composed of a concoction of honey, wheat and real blood—sometimes menstrual, but at other times not. From where then is it procured? "Animals" have been used, but there are other possibilities. As it says in the *Book of the Law*: "The best blood is of the moon, monthly (menses): then the fresh blood of a child...Sacrifice cattle, little and big: after a child."

One must probe deeply to determine whether or not the OTO practices blood sacrifice of human beings in the literal, commonly accepted sense. The practice is certainly not official, nor is it officially condoned. It may be confined to unstable persons who take Aleister Crowley at his word and act out the impulses he sanctions, against the overt, stated wishes of OTO leaders who issue plausible denials.

The Manson Family

The bloody slaughter on August 9, 1969 of actress Sharon Tate and four others shocked the world that year. The details of the murders are well-known, including stabbing Tate's unborn child and smearing the victims' blood on the wall to write "Helter Skelter," words which were the title of a Beatles song written one year after the Beatles had sparked a revival of interest in deceased OTO leader Aleister Crowley by placing his photo on the cover of their album, "Sgt. Pepper's Lonely Hearts Club Band."

Tate was the wife of film director Roman Polanski who had directed "Rosemary's Baby," a movie about a demonic "moonchild." In a secret instruction of the OTO's Ninth Degree, details are given regarding the creation of a moonchild or homunculus via demonic possession of the fetus following ritualized copulation. Southern California OTO leader Jack Parsons, whose lodge was deeply tied to Hollywood, had gone to great lengths to create a moonchild in the 1940s. Numerous abortions were involved in the process. Indeed, "Rosemary's Baby" could be legitimately viewed as a graphically symbolic enactment of a homunculus ritual on celluloid.

Many books have been written about the "Manson

murders," blaming Charles Manson's views on white racism and too many drug trips. His involvement with the Solar Lodge, however, is less well known. The successor to Parsons' Agape Lodge in Pasadena was located in southern California and numbered among its adherents a young man named Charles Manson.

OTO leader Grady McMurty ("Hymenaeus Alpha") contacted the FBI following Manson's arrest, explaining for the record that the lodge in which Manson had been initiated was not recognized by the OTO—just a lone bastard lodge all on its own. These denials are themselves controversial for, even within branches of the maze known as the OTO, there are others who would call McMurty a bastard himself and deny his lineage and authority. These multiple cross-denials and the chaos they engender serve to unbalance investigators and allow the advance of cryptic processes through misdirection. Beneath this sea of roiling waters however, the occult command hierarchy is intact and functioning.

The obscured fact beneath these "official" statements and denials of "recognition" is the possibility that through the Solar Lodge Manson was acquainted with the *Book of the Law* and its solid, literal basis for ritual murder. In the second chapter explaining the OTO's Law of Thelema ("Law of the Will"), Manson may have read these words: "Worship me with fire & blood...let blood flow to my name...Sacrifice...a child...Mercy let be off: damn them who pity! Kill and torture; spare not; be upon them!..."

Just as Crowley had been raised as a child within the fanatical Fundamentalist "Christian" sect known as the Plymouth Brethren, Manson may have acted as a Thelemic Fundamentalist and grasped the logic of the demands of the Will to Power as explained by Crowley.

Whatever the case with Manson, Satanic Ritual Murder exists, and can also be called Masonic Ritual Abuse and Mind Control experimentation as conducted by the so-called intelligence community, as in the infamous MK-ULTRA program of the CIA, in which drugs, psycho-surgery, lobotomy, electro-convulsive shock and hypnosis were tried on various "patients."

To give a few examples: in Germany on July 6, 2001, Daniel and Manuela Ruda stabbed Frank Hackert 66 times, cut a pentagram on his stomach, drank his blood from a bowl on an altar topped with skulls, and copulated in a silk-lined, oak coffin. In the same year in Leesburg, Virginia, Kyle Hulbert stabbed biophysicist Robert Schwartz to death with a sword, afterward drinking Schwartz's blood. In Brisbane in 1999, two teenagers calling themselves "the AntiChrist" and "the Angel of Sorrow" stalked a 59-year-old tourist in Noosa National Park, then stabbed her 22 times and cut her throat from ear to ear. In Helsinki in 1999, a man and teenage woman devoted to the occult tortured and suffocated a "friend," then sexually abused the body, ate parts of it, finally sawing it to pieces.

In Buenos Aires, in 1999, a 50-year-old man was mutilated by his two daughters, who belonged to an alchemical Order. They stabbed their father 100 times, carved symbols on his body and ate part of his face. In Warsaw, 1999; Eustis, Florida, 1996; Athens, 1995; and Brisbane, 1989, similar grisly acts were committed for similar motives by occult-minded men and women. Crowley's legacy is clearly not without progeny. Whether the preceding incidents reflect aberrant insanity, government mind control experiments or the occasional "virus" in the Group Mind factored in to the implanted occult programming of the populace, there is no question that they carry out the injunction of the *Book of the Law*: "Mercy let be off: damn them who pity! Kill and torture; spare not..."

But the real legacy of Manson and Crowley is already here: the Molech sacrifice of abortion, with its Talmudic sanction. [2]

Do we notice this legacy for what it is? If not, Crowley and his imitators have served well to deepen our trance and dictate to us "unacceptable" versus "acceptable" types of dismemberment of the innocent. As Crowley's "holy book" states, chapter Two verse 58, "The slaves shall serve."

---

[2] According to the Talmud , embryos less than 40 days old are considered as "mere water." After the first 40 days the unborn child may be killed if it has the rabbinic status of *rodef* ("pursuer").

Heavy Metal Military

The ritual OTO microcosm is parent to the OTO moonchild in macrocosm: American culture, with its increasing flirtation with Satanic imagery, blood, sex, nudity and sadism. So steeped in the occult is the current generation of American youngsters, that the U.S. military has taken to incorporating the "music" of "heavy metal" rock bands like the group with the androgynous, alchemical code name, "AC/DC" in its official psychological training programs and operations.

In April of 2004, U.S. commanders had troops blare "Hells Bells" by AC/DC at the Muslim population of Fallujua, Iraq. Journalists embedded with U.S. combat troops have remarked upon the ubiquity of this "music" among the young soldiers. "Rock music" once regarded as borderline Satanic is now common and accepted. In the same vein, at the Abu Ghraib prison in Iraq, U.S. soldiers forced Muslim men to strip naked and simulate degenerate sex acts upon one another. While these sordid actions were dismissed as those of a "few rotten apples," information has emerged testifying to the fact that these perverted poses were often made at the behest of U.S. Intelligence agents in the American military's chain of command. It should be noted that the acts imposed on Iraqi prisoners by members of the US military bear more than a passing resemblance to occult rituals.

Tarot Cards

When its leadership wished to spearhead a revival of the OTO in America, the Aleister Crowley Tarot deck was cleverly marketed. This colorful version of the *Book of Thoth* has been a favorite method of introducing youth to the OTO. It was produced by the U.S. Game Company, put into stores, and continues to sell in major bookstore chains. What teenager wouldn't at least pick up a deck of Tarot cards, particularly with the erotic art on the deck, painted by a certain "Lady" Frieda Harris under the direction of "Sir" Aleister Crowley?

What kid doesn't long to have a few powers and become a comic book hero and see into the future? And of course, with his curiosity stoked by the popular Harry Potter books and movies, he is doubly eager to get a head start on preparing for Hogwarts School of Witchcraft and Wizardry. What better way than a Tarot deck by the most famous *real* magician of modern times, Aleister Crowley?

These Tarot decks have been a great marketing tool by which the OTO leads the disenchanted young iconoclast to look for its deeper and darker materials, to ask the clerk behind the counter in the New Age bookstore if he knows about any OTO meetings, or to buy Crowley's book on the subject, *The Book of Thoth,* which explains how to get in touch with the OTO and ultimately, to make initial contact.

This method continues to be one doorway for many youth into the OTO. I recently witnessed two young bookstore employees sorting the Tarot decks behind the glass case in a major chain bookstore; upon fingering the OTO deck, the young girl said, "I love Crowley—Crazy Crowley, crazy Crowley; he's so crazy," like a hypnotized parrot. The public relations wizards of the OTO have made certain that "Crowleyanity" remains an enduring youth fad that never goes out of fashion.

But then there are those troubling passages about blood in the "holy book" of the OTO. The teen is told that these passages have nothing to do with murder; he is further told that the law of the OTO is the law of liberty, and that the OTO is not Satanic, and indeed tolerates all religions, although it believes that the era of Christianity is over.

Hatred and Bigotry Toward True Christians

This OTO hype is certainly less than candid. The OTO despises true Christians, considering them the repressive "Black Brothers" or "Black Lodge," the "slaves of the slave-gods" who need to be overthrown, ultimately by the "sword" as candid members will admit (quoting, for example, *Liber CCC*).

In an example of their hypocrisy, the OTO's indictment of intolerance in the Catholic Church and "organized religion" boomerangs against the OTO itself, which is, ironically, a tax-exempt organized religion in the United States, as it warms up to the subject in the most intolerant language possible. For instance, in *The Book of the Law* (3:49-55), we read:

"I am in a secret fourfold word, the blasphemy against all gods of men. Curse them! Curse them! Curse them! With my Hawk's head I peck at the eyes of Jesus as he hangs upon the cross. I flap my wings in the face of Mohammed & blind him. With my claws I tear out the flesh of the Indian and the Buddhist, Mongol and Din. Bahlasti! Ompehda! I spit on your crapulous creeds. Let Mary inviolate be torn upon wheels: for her sake let all chaste women be utterly despised among you!"

One apologist for these rabidly hateful words, Crowley's disciple Israel Regardie, explained them away by comparing them with a Zen master's saying, "If you meet the Buddha, slay him." Neophytes are told that this passage is a mere attempt to lead us beyond dogmas in a Zen-like manner, perhaps shocking us into enlightenment as a bonus.

The official OTO commentary to *The Book of the Law* is also strewn with outbursts such as "The Christians to the lions!" No doubt this is another Zen koan, not to be taken literally. It is difficult to find much credibility in such a position. [3]

In *The Vision and the Voice*, second only to The *Book of the Law* in importance within the OTO, we are regaled as follows:

"And Satan is worshipped by men under the name of Jesus; and Lucifer is worshipped by men under the name of Brahma; and Leviathan is worshipped by men under the name of Allah; and Belial is worshipped by men under the name of Buddha...Moreover, there is Mary, a blasphemy against BABALON, for she hath shut herself up; and therefore is she the Queen of all those wicked devils that walk upon the earth, those that thou sawest even as little black specks that stained the Heaven of

---

[3] Louis Wilkinson and Hymenaeus Beta, *The Law is for All: The Authorized Popular Commentary to The Book of the Law* (Tempe, Arizona: New Falcon Publications, 1996).

Urania. And all these are the excrement of Choronzon." [4]

Praising the "good intentions" of the apostate priests who perform Black Masses, the secret instructions for the Eighth Degree of the OTO tells us that these priests "set up Man against the foul demon of the Christians, and let this be accounted unto them for righteousness." The OTO prefers to hold its own version of a Mass, Gnostic rather than Black, rather than relying on any apostate Catholic priests (not that they are in short supply). The Gnostic Mass contains such rubrics as these: "She then holds it to her breast, while the PRIEST, falling at her knees, kisses them, his arms stretched along her thighs. He remains in this adoration while the DEACON intones the collects."

Children are routinely present during the Gnostic Mass. Although Crowley copied elements of the Catholic Mass in creating his Gnostic Mass, it contains obvious differences.

The OTO's pretense of tolerance is not only a con-game played within Masonic lodges, but reflects a much older model: the Synagogue and its "holy book," the Talmud, in which we read that Jesus is boiling in Hell in hot excrement (Gittin 57a) and that the best of the Gentiles should be killed (Soferim 15, Rule 10), while being told by smiling rabbis on television that Judaism is somehow connected with Christianity in a weird oxymoron known as "Judeo-Christianity,"a centaur-like infernal hybrid similar to the alchemical Man-Pig experiments of the Organ Farm Factory and modern genetic bio-engineering with transplants. The "Judeo-Christianity" of modern rabbis and church leaders is straight from the Island of Doctor Moreau.

Satanism

To touch a raw nerve in speaking with a member of the OTO, accuse the "Frater" or "Soror" of Satanism. The OTO takes great offense at the label. In a certain technical

---

[4] Tarot cards have become the basis of role-playing computer games. The OTO's pantheon has entered online computer-gaming culture by this means. Web-based computer games that "celebrate a decade of bloodletting" and feature the darkest of all OTO demons, Choronzon, are all over the aptly named web.

sense, perhaps it is correct to state that the OTO is not the same as classic Satanism, *if* Satanism is defined as a phenomenon of rebellion *per se* against Christianity which involves the ceremonial inversion of the Roman Catholic Mass in the form of the Black Mass. Crowley had higher, more modern ambitions; he wished not to simply rebel against Christianity but to replace it. Yet the note of rebellion is also present, and hence even in this antique sense Crowley emerges as a clearly Satanic figure. For example, in 1921, in Paris, Crowley recorded a "ceremony" which he performed as follows:

"A young cock is to be baptized Peter Paul into the Catholic church by C. J. A. Maitland, the son of an apostate Romish Priest, and therefore the ideal 'Black' Hierophant. Mary Butts and I are its sponsors. Peter and Paul are the founders of the Christian Church, and we want its blood to found our own church....I behead him (the cock), and the blood is caught in the silver 'charger' on the Disk. In this charger is the meal etc. for the Cakes of Light (communion wafers for the Gnostic Mass), ready except for the blood. I conjure the spirit of Peter Paul to serve these Cakes to found our Church with, as we may use them."

Crowley, in his *magnum opus* Book Four, establishes the OTO doctrine on Satanism in blatant, bombastic language: "Thou spiritual Sun! Satan, Thou Eye, Thou Lust! Cry aloud! Cry aloud! Whirl the Wheel, O my Father, O Satan, O Sun!...Give me such, Thou Phallus, Thou Sun! Satan, thou Eye, thou Lust! Satan, thou Eye, thou Lust! Satan, thou Eye, thou Lust! Thou self-caused, self-determined, exalted, Most High!...The Eye!

"Satan, my Lord! The Lust of the Goat! This serpent, SATAN, is not the enemy of Man, but He who made Gods of our race, knowing Good and Evil; He bade 'Know Thyself!' and taught Initiation. We have therefore no scruple in restoring the 'devil-worship' of such ideas as those which the laws of sound, and the phenomena of speech and hearing, compel us to connect with the group of 'Gods' whose names are based upon ShT, or D, vocalized by the free breath A. For these Names imply the qualities of courage, frankness, energy, pride, power and triumph; they are the words which express the creative and paternal will." [5]

In spite of the hardcore Satanic raving that flowed from Crowley's dogmatic writings like lava from hell, so contemptuous is the OTO of the intelligence of the general public that the public relations position of the OTO is that Satan-worship is not a requirement or even a widespread practice of the organization, but more of a personal choice, even claiming that Crowley wrote philo-Christian poetry, forgetting to inform the naive inquirer that Crowley said that he found the "Messiah" in "the Devil and all his angels." [6]

The OTO is technically correct in explaining away any OTO "requirement" of worshipping the devil, *under the name of Satan,* but obviously the preceding passages from Crowley's writings are a potent endorsement of the practice.

Moreover, the OTO understands that the symbol in the Tarot deck for the devil is the goat-headed figure called Baphomet, stemming from the 19th century drawing of the figure worshipped by the Knights Templars as rendered by Satanist Eliphas Levi (1810-1875). In the OTO's weekly Gnostic Mass, worshippers chant, "And I believe in the Serpent and the Lion, Mystery of Mystery, in His name BAPHOMET." After consecrating the elements in the Gnostic Mass into the "Body and Blood of God," the OTO priest genuflects and strikes his breast. The power of Baphomet is then invoked upon the worshippers present with the words, "O Lion and O Serpent that destroy the destroyer, be might among us."

This is said three times in place of the traditional *Agnus Dei* (Lamb of God) portion of the old Catholic Latin

---

[5] Crowley is here giving instruction on the worship of Shaitan (Satan) and Hadit, the winged solar disk which was a destructive form of Horus in Egyptian lore. His instruction is based on the importance of the vibrational sound of the words as reflected in the earliest edition of the kabbalistic book, *Sefer Yetzirah,* in which the exact pronunciation of syllables for several hours is required to invoke the entity known as the Golem.

[6] Aleister Crowley, *Why Jesus Wept,* privately printed, 1904 (see the section, "Dedicatio Extraordinaria").

Mass. In other words, the elements are adored as if they were God, and equated with the Lion and Serpent, who in turn is Baphomet, i.e. Satan. So, while these OTO cult-members do worship the devil at each of their Gnostic Mass ceremonies, in keeping with their heritage as heirs of the Father of Lies they deceptively hide Satan under a pile of code names. Prospective recruits participate in a Gnostic Mass without noticing any overt deviltry, only to learn much later that they have been worshipping Baphomet all along, at which point they are told not to worry, because he is not the enemy anyway. What a scam.

One of the founding tenets of the OTO is to shape and manage American popular culture, so that as a result we find a similar disguised Satanic symbolism peering out from the edges of our consumer utopia. When it dawns on us that our participation in this commerce constitutes a form of demonic idolatry, we are told "not to worry," American culture is not the enemy.

All of these conflicting messages, from the affirmation and contempt for life, to the denial and exaltation of blood and death, to the indignation over and immersion in Satanism, are understandable if we realize that Baphomet is an androgynous figure standing for the Double Mind, as well as two-faced duplicity. Navigating the OTO in particular and the occult in general is confusing for most investigators because they fail to grasp this fact.

Rank-and-file Freemasons who think they are sailing in a different fishing boat should take a good look at the inverted pentagram on the wall of their lodge; if they will care to consult their own leaders' writings (such as Albert Pike in *Morals and Dogma*), they will see that the inverted pentagram does not refer to the "Eastern Star" of Christ, but rather to the Androgynous and Double-Minded Goat of Baphomet, and is always a symbol of Black Magick.

The OTO is the domain of Baphomet: the intensification of the contradictions of the Masonic Brotherhood. In this fact it mirrors the consumer culture its brilliant architects have shaped: enormous, cathedral-like shopping shrines and computerized, virtual reality fantasy-role games, where murder according to Crowley's formula is just another option in a do-your-own-thing matrix.

III

The Beast 666

"Kill and torture; spare not; be upon them!"

Given the fact that the OTO is a worldwide, active secret society or cult, the reader is probably wondering about the goals of the organization. Is it simply a collection of odd occultists? A group of eccentrics with a penchant for sex and Satan, Eros and Horus? Are they harmless folk who like to talk a bit rough, scaring themselves with a few documents about blood and pushing the envelope by breaking the taboo on Devil worship if they are in the mood, but all in all, just one more group of existential moderns and understandably disgruntled ex-Christians — rebelling against childhood repression—but just as likely to help an old lady across the street as any Boy Scout or Brixton Baptist?

Some of the members are nostalgic for the '60s, reveling in drugs and debauchery; still fascinated with a pentagram and a pot plant. Such members are typically used for sex magick by those who know how; hence, the "Lodge Hippies" have their convenient place, are welcomed, vampirized, and viewed as dispensable.

Not every OTO member has green hair, a nose ring, and a case of Herpes, however. Some are scientists and physicians at the top of their fields, but the Left-wing of the OTO does believe that the entire "sexually-repressed" order of civilization based on Christian principles must be overthrown. Former OTO initiate and occult scholar Peter R. Koenig writes, "Lurking on the threshold of History, Thelema wants to communicate its ideas to the world. It evangelizes with the ultimate aim of destroying society's standards. It strives for world dominion and compares itself to the young Christianity that had been hunted by Rome. They say that 'If one were to substitute O.T.O. for Army, this would work very well for the Order." [1]

---

[1] P.R. Koenig, "Halo of Flies" in Richard Metzger, *Book of Lies: The Disinformation Guide to Magick and the Occult*, p. 253.

Eventually, this goal will, according to the OTO, require bloodshed. In *Khabs Am Pekht,* an official document, the OTO instructs members that "sooner or later we are to break the power of the slaves of the slave-gods by actual fighting. Ultimately, Freedom must rely upon the sword. It is impossible to treat in this epistle of the vast problems involved in this question; and they must be decided in accordance with the Law of the OTO, called Thelema) by those in authority in the Order when the time comes."

This passage is a commitment to a war against Christians "when the time comes," and since the OTO spans the globe from Croatia and Italy to Japan, New Zealand and South America, Christians might wish to inquire a bit further.

The OTO leader in England, Kenneth Grant, seeks a similar harrowing destiny. As Robert Anton Wilson notes, "Grant's version of the OTO lays heavy emphasis on anal variations of sex magick and on dark hints about long-range political objectives known only to the inner circle..." [2]

Grant himself declares: "The scientist, Wilhelm Reich, was eliminated by the American authorities because the logical conclusion of his discoveries implied the total overthrow of society as it is known today. Yet it is upon the debris of that society alone that the Kingdom of Ra-Hoor-Khuit may be established. The keen and persistent practice of Thelema by even a few dedicated individuals will effectually overthrow society..."

Similar grandiose aims are stated in the "Secret Instructions of the Seventh Degree," wherein the initiate is told, "And in what time seemeth Him good shall the O.H.O. (Outer Head of the Order), gathering his forces, declare this Truth privily unto the Kings and Princes of the Earth, that they may take counsel together and rule all men in peace and love by virtue of this Secret under the Shadow of the Wings of the One ineffable Lord."

Note the grotesque lie at the heart of the propaganda: Crowley's blood-soaked rule is presented as a *Weltanschauung* of peace and love! Here is the command

---

[2] Robert Anton Wilson, *Everything is Under Control: Conspiracies, Cults, and Cover-Ups*, p. 212.

ideology of the shepherds of Hermas who covertly shaped and managed the New Age and hippie movements from the 1960s onward, and whose popular symbol among the young was the Ankh Cross, a device whose original function in ancient Egypt was as a sheep tether.

Philosopher Thomas Molnar penetrated the cover story by seeing in the fabled "Abbey of Thelema," a clandestine counterchurch that advertised itself as the path to a liberating, do-your-own-thing utopia, free of rigid Church discipline and strictures. Molnar demonstrated however, that Thelema was in actuality a counter-church with rules even more rigid than that of the Christian Church, and the first glimmer of this diabolical bait-and-switch appeared during the French Revolution. Molnar made the startling comment, "Our civilization will no doubt come to an end the day the Catholic Church and the United States join the revolution."

Right Wing Conspiracy

In the furtherance of this goal Thelemicists planted the seeds of destruction on both Christianity's Left wing (the "ecumenists" and "conciliarists") *as well as on its right wing* (the "traditionalists"), in a process known in alchemy as *coincidentia oppositorum* ("coincidence of opposites").

Much has been written about occult infiltration coming from the Left; but most analysts have failed to investigate and expose subversion playing on Right wing tastes and affinities. Yet secret societies have a record of manipulating both sides of the human psyche and persona, shepherding those who crave egalitarianism and anarchy, as well as those who seek elite standards and authority.

Nicholas DeVere is the leader of a cult of which seeks to address the very real crisis of authority which afflicts the modern man who is haggard with doubt. DeVere's rhetoric is strikingly similar to the arguments of Christian traditionalists. DeVere rails against the "stupid New Age attitude" which "stems from the ridiculous, totally indefensible greed-driven free market assertion that anyone can become anything they choose, and the totally unfounded PC notion that everyone is equal."

It is easy to see that DeVere is no Leftist. His statements are music to traditionalist ears. He continues:

"This kind of pathetic liberalism, born as a reaction to the socially inculcated victim mentality, should be abhorred by all rational beings, and so my attitude towards...a great social leveler and equalizer is one of contempt. However, you don't make lots of money by telling the bulk of your readership that they are genetically excluded from a process they cannot experience or understand; you sell New Age drivel by telling the ingenuous that they can all assume any role they like, and adopt any trendy 'lifestyle' choice that whim and deceitful advertising dictates...." [3]

Who is Nicholas DeVere? Tridentine Mass lay leader? Conservative philosopher? Not quite. DeVere is a confessed Satanist and Luciferian: "At the age of twelve, Nicholas was magically dedicated to the dragon tradition formally, and at the age of thirteen he first enacted the rite known as 'Starfire.' Following this period his mother obtained for him works by Aleister Crowley, and he studied the principals of the Black Arts in earnest, gaining a considerable degree of competence in ritual magic. At the age of fifteen Nicholas underwent the ancient rite of kingship which, in accordance with archaic Gaelic tradition, bestows the mantle of sovereignty arising from the very Earth itself." [4]

DeVere demarcates his own place in the Crowley/OTO hierarchy: "...The contemporary Dragon Court is furthermore a combination of what Aleister Crowley would term several 'currents,' of which the major external one to the family proper was bestowed via the Black Country Covenant of the Baphometic Order of the Cubic Stone, who trace their origins back to the Knights Templar. This was given in recognition of my family's hereditary involvement in Royal Witchcraft and the historical Dragon tradition. Other external currents derive from the Knighthood of the Plantagenet Clan Donnachaid, Dragon cousins to the House of Vere, and laterally from Dr. John Dee's 'School of Night', of which Edward de Vere, the seventeenth earl of Oxford, was a prominent member. Edward also performed

---

[3] http://www.paranoiamagazine.com/mykingdom.html

[4] "Prince Nicholas de Vere von Drakenberg: A Short Biography" http://www.dagobertsrevenge.com/devere/bio.html

the rites of Dragon kingship in the family, specifically the rite of the kingship of the Calle Daouine." [5]

In *The Beginning of the New World,* Crowley outlined his authentic masterplan for those inclined toward Right wing authoritarianism: "The first practical step towards this end is the formation of a strong central organization to direct coherently the activities of the numerous adherents already established in many countries. It will then be necessary to convene conferences of experts in all the sciences, which treat of mankind in his social and individual character, in order to draw up a comprehensive international program." [6]

Instead of the vaunted libertarian utopianism we hear about from the average stoned Thelemite at a "rave" party, we see that the OTO can and will operate as a "strong central organization."

Those who were close to Crowley knew that he was a control-freak and the worst type of proto-fascist. The OTO's appeal and one of the primary reasons it is so dangerous is that it is the heir to Satanic knowledge of human psychology. The fact is, Crowley's followers are found on the extreme Right, among people psychologically disposed toward royalism, authoritarianism and elaborate ceremonies and pageantry.

This has been true of the 20th century occult generally, though the OTO perfected the process. Here we enter one of the most difficult and recondite areas of study in the entire realm of counter-intelligence, the stratagem of the "black op" or false front that alchemically serves to unite opposites. One of the most dazzling examples of this may be found in a book published in 2004, *The Slaves Shall Serve* by James Wasserman, one of the most brilliant and erudite of all OTO leaders. *The Slaves Shall Serve* is a major statement by the OTO.

This book marks the opening of a new and daring public appeal to the American Right Wing. The author

---

[5] http://www.paranoiamagazine.com/mykingdom.html

[6] "The Beginning of the New World," in Aleister Crowley, *The Revival of Magick and Other Essays* (Tempe: New Falcon Publications, 1998).

credits the John Birch Society openly, while stating that he is "not a member for personal reasons." He recommends reading William Jasper, John McManus and John Birch Society texts, together with *Liber Oz*, "a statement published by the English master Aleister Crowley during World War II, presents what I consider to be the ideal statement of the political rights of any individual courageous enough to live up to the responsibilities freedom entails."

Wasserman attacks the Muslims in John Birch Society language, as "Islamo-fascism" and supposedly champions "liberty," using Birch arguments against the United Nations. Wasserman reprints a considerable portion of Birch material on the UN and annotates it as well, showing the UN to be a problem--in part. He of course doesn't go into the UN's role in the founding of Israel, nor the murderous UN sanctions against Iraq but not Israel, nor the UN's relationship to Freemasonry (going back to the failed League of Nations sponsored by the Grand Orient and other Lodges). That's the cunning utility of telling the "partial truth."

What is going on here? The OTO perceives that the conspiracy spotlight needs to be kept off both Judaism and Freemasonry--the OTO being based on the Kabbalah--and therefore they place opprobrium mainly on Islam and promote those groups, like John Birch, who do likewise. The OTO, having corrupted the culture through channels consonant with the "Left," is now positioning itself to steer the kosher conservative "Right."

We note that Wasserman denies that Islamic resistance is tied to US support for Israel. He urges Americans to join the NRA, and carries footnote after footnote from *The New American*, including the questionable claim that the Oklahoma City bombing was linked to the Arabs. The OTO leader even endorses Judge Roy Moore, arguing that American institutions should publicly exhibit the Ten Commandments. Coming from an active OTO member, this statement would be risible were it not a sobering indication of something deeply subversive at work.

Wasserman further states that a belief in a Higher Power is a guarantee of freedom. In his footnote to this statement he proceeds to advise the "Younger Brethren" to come out of their "swoon" and recall their pursuit of the "HGA" and all will be well. What is this "HGA" that the youth should pursue? "HGA" is an OTO code for "Holy Guardian Angel," which Crowley teaches in Book Four to invoke as, "Satan, Thou Lust!"

The concern about "Muslim pursuit of world domination" is that it will usurp OTO pursuit of world domination. (One of the leaders in the OTO is called "Caliph" and even wears a turban). As for advocating the posting of the Ten Commandments, what a revelation! Thelemites are *dead set against all Ten.* Wasserman even tries to explain that when he quotes *Liber Oz* by Crowley, who writes, "there is no god but man," that such a statement doesn't make Wasserman an atheist because of the "superconscious" in man being God.

The OTO is a force shaping the Right. This point is very significant. The OTO believes that the John Birch Society is a highly useful vehicle for distracting attention away from Judaism to Islam, and away from Masonry to the United Nations.

Mr. Wasserman, an agent of the New World Order, writes, "Invaluable data on the history and nature of the internationalist tyranny is provided by John McManus in *Financial Terrorism,* William Jasper in *Global Tyranny,* and *The United Nations Exposed,* and James Perloff in *Shadows of Power.* These four books discuss the New World Order in frightening but sane detail. They are well-researched, and scrupulously annotated with source materials from the public record. *Global Tyranny* contains a humorous chapter on the New Age movement that displays considerable ignorance--but we can separate the wheat from the chaff, can we not? In fact, much of the criticism he (Jasper) raises about the New Age movement is accurate. He describes it as having been co-opted by left wing activists camouflaging their true agenda in eco-spiritual terms. Gorbachev and his ilk as the high priests of a socialist cult disguised as paganism, whose actual purpose is the Marxist goal of eliminating private property." [7]

Wasserman recommends to the reader the "authorized OTO commentary on the *Book of the Law*," namely *The Law is For All*. In that work Crowley is explicit about government needing to have a class of elites and most people needing to be slaves. In fact, the title of Wasserman's book, *The Slaves Shall Serve*, is actually an inside-joke since it is a quote from Crowley's *Book of the Law*.

Wasserman's enthusiasm for the Birch attack on the United Nations is passing strange in view of the historical role of the OTO in the founding of the New World Order, and of the record of Wasserman's esteemed paladin, Aleister Crowley, in this regard. The OTO played its role in the general milieu which spawned the hype clamoring for what H.G. Wells called the "World State." If one seeks for nursemaids and midwives for the UN's predecessor, the League of Nations, the OTO should also not be overlooked. Crowley was employed from 1915 to 1917 by George Sylvester Viereck, editor of the influential journals, *The Fatherland* and *The International*. Three years before the founding of the League of Nations, Crowley was writing in this vein for *The International:* "Let the lower interest be betrayed to the higher, the particular benefit of any given country to the Commonwealth of the whole world." The UN's Temple of Understanding contains a stained-glass window of the goat-footed god Pan, Crowley's greatest and first love besides himself.

The following statements concerning Wasserman were online in October, 2004 at the website of the Sekhet-Maat Lodge of the OTO: "James Wasserman joined Ordo Templi Orientis in 1976. In 1979, he founded Tahuti Lodge, one of the oldest continuous O.T.O. Lodges in the world. He has played a key role in numerous seminal publications of the Crowley literary corpus. Three of these include his supervision of Weiser's 1976 edition of *The Book of the Law*, in which the holograph manuscript was appended to the corrected typeset text of the O.T.O.'s 1938 publication -- in conformity with the book's instructions for the first

[7] James Wasserman, *The Slaves Shall Serve*, p. 105.

time in a popular volume. After several years of negotiation, he successfully arranged to professionally re-photograph the Crowley/Harris Tarot paintings for an improved second edition of the Thoth Tarot deck published in 1977, to which he contributed the Booklet of Instruction. In 1983, he worked with two other members of the O.T.O. to produce *The Holy Books of Thelema*, a collection of Crowley's inspired (Class A) writings.

"In 1986, his essay entitled 'An Introduction to the History of the O.T.O.' was published in *Equinox III*, No. 10...In 1989, he described his adaptation of the Middle Pillar exercise to group workings in Israel Regardie's *Healing Energy, Prayer and Relaxation* (New Falcon Publications). In 1992, he wrote and designed *Art and Symbols of the Occult*, a beautiful, full-color overview of the primary disciplines and images of the occult tradition (Inner Traditions). In 1993, he compiled, edited and wrote an extensive introduction for *Aleister Crowley and the Practice of the Magical Diary* (New Falcon Publications, reissued 2003 by Sekmet Books). In 1994, after 15 years of development, his groundbreaking edition of *The Egyptian Book of the Dead* was published by Chronicle Books. The book features a magnificent color reproduction of the Papyrus of Ani with an integrated English translation. In 1996, he designed, edited, and wrote an Afterword for Aleister Crowley's important mystical poem *AHA!* (New Falcon Publications).

"In 2001, *The Templars and the Assassins: The Militia of Heaven,* the result of over seven years research and writing, was published by Inner Traditions. Already translated into four languages, it appears to be well on its way to becoming a modern classic on the subject of the holy warrior. The book eerily anticipated the September 11 attacks that occurred just four months after its publication."

The focus of Wasserman's *Templars and Assassins* book was to re-emphasize the era of the Crusades and its imagery, in line with the propaganda being served up since 9/11. *The Slaves Shall Serve* extends this operation by layering on Conservative, neo-con propaganda to stir in a hard swerve to the Right by the OTO, which is clearly returning to its roots in Reuss and other well-dressed "lords."

The Templars and the Assassins was endorsed by the head of the Golden Dawn, the head of the Temple of Set, and one of the heads of another occult order. The triple-teaming of these groups is unprecedented. The cover depicts the Templars dressed in inverted colors fighting Arabs. What is our supposed "Christian West" today, but an inverted crusade, a pseudo-"Christian" Crusade on behalf of Judaic supremacy and Zionist hegemony? The book's cover illustration shows the Arabs and Crusaders battling over a wall which is crumbling and fades into two towers. Behind them are two Arab assassins--the Diable, and Usama/Osama, beneath two stars (presumably intended to symbolize Sirius A and Sirius B from the constellation Canis major).

Targeting Traditional Catholics

Another case in point is the significant enthusiasm for the old traditional Catholic, Latin "Tridentine" Mass among Right-wing occultists. Among these enthusiasts, C.W. Leadbeater is perhaps most notorious. A former Anglican priest and associate of the occult "theosophist" (gnostic) Helena Blavatsky, "Leadbeater was nevertheless aware that the magic of the Christian sacraments was still very much needed by contemporary humanity...

"In such works as The Science of the Sacraments, The Inner Side of Christian Festivals and his recently and posthumously published The Christian Gnosis, he left an impressive legacy wherein he demonstrated to the satisfaction of many that the Mass and other sacraments of apostolic Christendom are capable of assisting the spiritual welfare and transformative growth of persons in our age..."

The OTO has exploited the fact that certain occultists "valued the Western spiritual traditions, such as ceremonial magic, esoteric masonry, and the mystery and sacred magic of the Christian sacraments....Many ...theosophists also became attracted to the stately beauty and mysticism of the Mass and the other sacraments...To say that there could be an occult Catholicism is not as absurd as some might think. History teems with prelates, priests, and nuns of the Catholic Church who were devoted and skilled occultists. Kabbalah, hermeticism, astrology and magic were all patronized...Even today, one may discover that persons of gnostic-hermetic interests have more in common with traditionalist Catholics than with either modernist Vatican II Catholics or with Protestants." [8]

This is not to say that the Catholic Tridentine Rite itself is occult. On the contrary, it has stood for centuries as a bulwark against the diabolic attempt to twist Jesus Christ into a Gnostic/pagan archetype. Leftist occult conspirators in the Vatican suppressed the Tridentine Mass in 1969 with the zeal of a Thomas Cranmer, while Rightist occult conspirators seek to control the remnant who are attracted to it in the wake of the suppression.

Confusing? Not if one possesses a key gnosis, what the Zohar terms the "knowledge of the equilibrium." Just as Voodoo practitioners use Catholic trappings, statues and other paraphernalia to pervert Catholicism into a magical superstition, the Right-wing of the conspiracy exploits a superstition among some Catholics who hold to a kind of unspoken "magical sacramentalism," i.e. the notion that being present at the Holy Mass itself, with its awe-inspiring solemnity and its bells, incense and candles; and not one's state of grace, fidelity to the Commandments of God or relationship with Jesus Christ -- becomes the individual's guarantor of sanctity.

If the Mass is a kind of magic, as stated by a seminary lecturer and prominent writer for the largest "traditional" Catholic group in America, then the priest must be a magician.

This "magical sacramentalism" falsifies the reality of the Eucharist and Satanically mocks it, by twisting it into a totem of the eternal pagan psychodrama, rather than upholding the truth that, as the embodiment of Calvary, the Eucharist is the sole ontological exception to that psychodrama.

I hasten to add that this perverted magical belief is *not* intrinsic to Catholicism. Rather, it is just that, a Satanic perversion. Pope Pius V convened the Council of Trent in

---

[8] Stephan A. Hoeller, *Gnosis Magazine*, Vol. 12, Summer 1989. (Hoeller is *not* a member of the OTO).

part to crush this heretical counterfeit theology, a function of the "Satan is the ape of God" process. The crisis today is that orthodox, authentically traditional Catholics too often do not wish to confront this growing menace in their ranks, preferring instead to sweep it under the rug, which is exactly what the occult infiltrators hope they will do.

The occult heresy of magical sacramentalism and the aristocratic caste mentality it fosters reflects the hierarchical order Crowley sought to impose. The model Crowleyian hierarchy has no accountability. A megalomaniac does not brook interference. Checks and balances are nonexistent. The goal is absolute power without restraint.

Where better to launch such a totalitarian project than in the ranks of "breakaway" traditional Catholics who crave the restoration of order and obedience, but who do not recognize any higher earthlyauthority other than the prelates who rule over theirparticular group?

Blasphemous Royalism:
Priory of Sion; Da Vinci Code

Magical sacramentalism is not the only means for transforming pious Catholics into slavish occultists. If we study the juncture at which royalism and monarchism intersect with the once secret heresy which teaches that certain of the crowned heads of Europe were literal genetic descendants of Jesus Christ, we begin to discern the emergence of an organization that would have an authority so divine it could not be resisted by any believing Christian. The lure of this hallucination to occultists seeking to impose totalitarian rule is nearly irresistible. Their modern agent in this regard was Pierre Plantard (1920-2000), the supposed scion of the ancient Merovingian king, Dagobert II.

Plantard was the 20th century godfather of the "Priory of Sion" mythos which claims that certain royal families of Europe are the descendants of a fabled sexual union between Jesus and Mary Magdalene.

In 1942, Plantard founded the Alpha Galates. "The Alpha Galates was a Right Wing, Anti-Semitic, esoteric Roman Catholic Group that was clearly representative of the French Tradition known as the Grand Occident – in contrast to the Grand Orient that was pro-Republican in nature. The Tradition of the Grand Occident developed into various Orders of Right-Wing Knighthoods by the period of the German Occupation of France."

Not everyone was gulled by the front, however. The World War Two-era French journal *Au Pilori* accused Plantard's Order of being Freemasonic in nature, by revealing its grades of initiation and referring to Plantard as "His Druidic Majesty": "*We express our admiration, with complete impartiality, for this new Order of Chivalry, and wish His Druidic Majesty every success in the accomplishment of his Work.*" [9]

The *Au Pilori* writer was on to something. The leading traditional Roman Catholic group in the West today has been funded in part by European nobility and can be superficially described in nearly the same terms as the Alpha Galates: right-wing, esoteric and anti-Jewish. This group in its public pronouncements is staunchly anti-Judaic, but like the slippery Plantard, upon closer examination it is subtly connected to a Kabbalah-style mindset and sects of very shadowy provenance. Head-turning contradictions and dizzying alliances with seemingly completely opposed organizations and personnel abound.

The con-man Plantard was running one such false front decades ago. But his was no ordinary con. Plantard's network was operating within both Conservative Catholic and anti-Jewish circles, while also organizing and inspiring Kabbalist and "goddess" affiliates.

Plantard's most spectacular success in this regard was the Priory of Sion's influence on Dan Brown, author of the devilishly effective publishing phenomenon, *The Da Vinci Code,* with ten million copies in print. With *The Da Vinci Code* the intrigue has assumed global proportions.

The macabre irony is that the Priory of Sion, the "order of chivalry" allegedly created in 1099 by the "Crusader Godefroy de Bouillon" has become, via the Catholic Pierre Plantard and the New Age Dan Brown, the transmission belt for the revival of the witchcraft cult of Isis, the black

---

[9] *Au Pilori,* November 19, 1942.

magic of the Kabbalah and filthy Talmudic sexual libel against Jesus Christ.

Perhaps now the reader is beginning to gain insight into the utility of the OTO's specialty, what Dr. Carl Gustav Jung termed *Mysterium Coniunctionis* (the synthesis of psychic opposites in alchemy). The OTO does not wish to direct only the Left-wing "progressive" drive for "modernization and reform" and leave the Right wing opposition in the hands of its enemies.

Rather, the OTO is always and everywhere determined to impose the Kabbalistic paradigm by *controlling the opposition*. The OTO appeals to elite standards of culture and taste in upholding the classic liturgies, even as Vatican agents inspired by the OTO zeitgeist outlawed these rites for general use.

In this limited sense, the conspiracy has been quite successful. Tridentine Mass attendance is nowadays limited to small pockets of Catholics who, as targets of occult infiltration, are more susceptible to penetration than a mass movement consisting of millions of believers would be.

Here we are reminded of the ancient alchemical dictum, *Solve et coagula* ("break down and re-form"). The Tridentine Mass of yore sanctified countless clergy and laity and some of the most beloved saints of the Church.

But the hundreds of millions of people devoted to it were -- with remarkable dispatch -- stripped away almost in the twinkling of an eye, with the long-term objective of creating a new, much more circumscribed Tridentine Mass movement rigidly controlled by the occult. [10]

---

[10] This writer and other investigators have compiled evidence of occult agents making inroads into the Traditional Mass movement in the U.S in the past twelve years. It should be noted, however, that many traditional Catholics have -- thus far -- remained free of these connections and would be horrified if they were to learn of them. A similar struggle occurred in the Church centuries ago, between advocates of the Council of Trent, from which the name "Tridentine" is derived, and Renaissance-humanist advocates of a "Christian Kabbalah."

"Do What Thou Wilt" Liberty Scam

While the OTO preaches the "Law of Liberty" as a cover-story, it simultaneously proclaims political and societal goals which are opposed to the very root of freedom. The schizophrenia attendant on these contradictions and the mentality that entertains them is excruciating in its rationalizations. One official OTO text comments that "...it is necessary for the development of Freedom itself to have an organization; and every organization must have a highly-centralized control. This is especially necessary in time of war, as even the so-called 'democratic' nations have been taught by Experience, since they would not learn from Germany. Now this age is pre-eminently a 'time of war,' most of all now, when it is our Work to overthrow the slave-gods." [11]

The Crowley/OTO organizational power trip is contrasted to ill effect with their libertarian propaganda. The Great Beast himself states that, "The Book of the Law was given to mankind chiefly in order to provide it with an impeccable principle of practical politics...We should have no compunction in utilizing the natural qualities of the bulk of mankind. We do not insist on trying to train sheep to hunt foxes or lecture on history; we look after their physical well being, and enjoy their wool and mutton. In this way we shall have a contented class of slaves who will accept the conditions of existence as they really are, and enjoy life with the quiet wisdom of the cattle."

This OTO might-is-right doctrine comes to the fore in the analysis of Crowley's extremely slippery relationship with Nazism. In 1915 Crowley wrote, "The world-head of the OTO is a German; and it is up to the OTO to rebuild the civilizations of Europe. It can only be done the German way. The day of the flannelled fool is over." Although Crowley was an agent of British Intelligence, he savored Hitler's hypnotic charisma and viewed him as marshaling part of the forces that were smashing the old repressive Christian Order—the "Aeon of Osiris."

The OTO was eventually suppressed in Nazi Germany,

---

[11] Aleister Crowley: *The Law is for All: The Authorized Popular Commentary to The Book of the Law.* (Tempe: New Falcon Publications, 1996), .p. 37.

chiefly because of OTO leader Karl Germer's connection with British Agent Crowley, who was viewed as a rival. The Germans of the Hitler era had their own Teutonic occult orders anyway, including the Ordo Novi Templi, or Order of the New Templars (ONT), which assisted the rise of the National Socialist German Worker's Party (*Nationalsozialistische Deutsche Arbeiter Partei*, or NSDAP—i.e "Nazi" party). The Germanen Order, an ONT offshoot, may have been the prototype for the Thule Society, a pagan/occult organization which also lent support to the NSDAP.

In the post-World War I wreckage that was Germany, it was almost inevitable that occult-pagan revivalism would grow, and that such elements would attach themselves to any prominent movement, including National Socialism, yet it is also true that one could not be a member of the Nazi party and a Freemason, since Hitler feared the Judaic predominance in the lodges.

Nevertheless, one of the ultimate historical ironies of Adolf Hitler's legacy is the fact that he came to embody aspects of the philosophy of these very lodges which he had denounced, mirroring Zionist racialism with his own Aryan racialism, and lodge secrecy and oppression with his Gestapo and myriad other secret police bureaus. In the final analysis, no one helped the cause of Zionism more than Hitler through his heavy-handed and tragically oppressive measures against Judaics, which have been mythologized into an eternally enshrined justification of Israeli supremacy, packaged in the emotive-religious term "holocaust." The Fuehrer, the great opponent of Zionism, could rightly be called, by way of resulting reaction, the father of the Israeli state.

Crowley's contradictory statements on Germans and Judaics can be reconciled through insight into the contradictions within Hitler himself and the predictable results of his persecutions of "Jews." Crowley wrote, in a marginal gloss in his own copy of his collection of poems, *The Giant's Thumb* (forward, p. xxi): "My life for England..." And in his revealing essay, "An Open Letter to Rabbi Joel Blau," Crowley declared, "Let the Jew lead the way!" He adds that the (Judaic) "Messiah must arise, and

His name shall be called Anti-Christ..." [12]

Then as now, the OTO. was playing both sides: offering enthusiasm for Hitler's bloodshed and wars and, as an agent of Britain's MI6 secret police and British Freemasonry, simultaneously supporting Zionism.

Crowley preached occult fascism, venerated Adolf Hitler *and* Rabbi Blau, and remained a British agent and crypto-Zionist all of his life. In his autobiography, Crowley has many catty things to say about Jewish persons, rather like the mutterings of a snobbish proprietor of an exclusive country club. Harry Truman is known to have also cast aspersions on some Judaics in private conversation as well, but few served the Cryptocracy more obediently than 33rd degree Freemason Harry S. Truman, and this can be said of Crowley too.

Crowley came to head the OTO after being recruited from the ranks of Freemasonry. In his own words: "Although I was admitted to the thirty-third and last degree of [Scottish Rite] Freemasonry so long ago as 1900, it was not until the summer of 1912 that my suspicion was confirmed. I speak of my belief that behind the frivolities and convivialities of our greatest institution (Freemasonry) lay in truth a secret. But at the time I speak of, a man came to me, a man of those mysterious masters of esoteric Freemasonry who are alike its Eyes and its Brains, and who exist in its midst—unknown, often, even to its acknowledged chiefs...This man had been watching my occult career for some years, and deemed me now worthy to partake in the Greater Mysteries." [13]

The man who approached Crowley was "Frater Merlin," (Theodor Reuss), from whom Crowley later obtained leadership of the OTO. Crowley attained the Baphomet XI degree, the "Supreme and Holy King of Ireland, Iona, and all the Britains that are in the Sanctuary of the Gnosis, OTO." When Crowley became the OHO or Outer Head of the Order, relatively sensible Germans in the OTO refused

---

[12] Aleister Crowley, *The Revival of Magic and Other Essays,* pp. 151-154.

[13] Kenneth Grant, *Aleister Crowley and the Hidden God,* p. 174.

to follow him. Crowley had also begun to leak secrets of his earlier Rosicrucian Magickal Order, the Hermetic Order of the Golden Dawn—founded by a group of high-ranking Freemasons.

But Crowley's role is, to his followers, more than a mere promoter of esoteric trivia. To them, Crowley was the Logos of the New Aeon of Horus, which began in 1904 with Crowley's "reception" of *The Book of the Law,* dictated to him over three days in Cairo, Egypt. Although every Masonic lodge had traditionally boasted a "Book of the Law" upon an altar—one of the "Landmarks" of Freemasonry--the typical "Book of the Law" had little to do with Freemasonry in its essence, changing as it did with the religion of the initiate. Hence, a Christian initiate swears upon a Bible; a Muslim Mason upon a Koran, such are the typical Books of the Law in any ordinary lodge. But with Crowley's revelation, dictated to him by "Aiwass," identified by Crowley as Satan and by Kenneth Grant as an alien discarnate intelligence, Freemasonry at last had a binding Book of the Law which was incumbent on all Freemasons of whatever branch.

Crowley "channeled" a Law codified in a book which he claimed was revealed by his "Guardian Angel," the demon Aiwass, the Law of Thelema based on the Rabelais-derived maxim, "Do what thou wilt shall be the whole of the Law."

In 1904, the scenario painted by the Book of the Law was unthinkable: a society based not on cynical lip-service to Christian principles, but on the willing embrace of their opposite: on self-actualization instead of self-sacrifice; on adultery and every conceivable form of sexual expression and license; on drug use, occultism; on extolling widespread war and bloodshed; and on a Darwinian advocacy of the elimination of the weak. Yet the past century has, following Crowley's prophetic reception of the "dictation," actually witnessed the incarnation of these very concepts in gargantuan proportions. Was the OTO correct—had some discarnate intelligence "tipped his hand" and announced his plan for the Twentieth Century to his innermost circle of Masonic followers—the OTO? Is the *Book of the Law,* as some have insisted, the blueprint of Satan for a world without God?

In 1907, Captain J. F. C. Fuller of the Oxfordshire Light

Infantry (later a key architect of British military strategy
in World War II) met Crowley for the first time and
subsequently wrote an encomium entitled *The Star in the
West,* in which appeared a term of his own invention,
"Crowleyanity."

Initially, Crowley had made his appearance as a poet,
reviewed favorably, at first, by G. K. Chesterton (of whom
Crowley once wrote, "with you I choose to measure
myself...you are a force to be reckoned with...whether we
are indeed friends or enemies it is perhaps hard to say").
Crowley began to try his prolific hand at prose as well,
churning out a monumental outpouring. His influence
began to grow. James Branch Cabell borrowed Crowley's
Gnostic Mass for Chapter 22 of his work *Jurgen.* And W.
Somerset Maugham, the world renowned novelist, based
the electrifying character of Oliver Haddo on Crowley in
the sensational 1908 book *The Magician,* which features
alchemy, a homunculus and Haddo's bewitching power
over the virginal Margaret. Like Crowley, Maugham too
was a British Intelligence agent. Maugham's novel,
Ashenden was the basis of Alfred Hitchcock's 1936 film,
"The Secret Agent."

Haddo-like, Crowley seduced a string of women for his
sex-and-sorcery rites, such as Leila Waddell, Leah Hirsig
and many others, along with homosexually-inclined men.
In 1910 at Caxton Hall in England, Crowley mounted one
of the first drug parties of modern times, serving
hallucinogenic mushrooms mixed with rotten-smelling
apples to his audience. Crowley anticipated and pioneered
virtually every facet of the hippie and New Age
movements that would emerge from under his shadow
half-a-century later.

In 1920 an "Abbey of Thelema" was built in Cefalu,
Sicily and Crowley held his OTO ceremonies there, until
his operation was shut down and he was ordered out of the
country by Benito Mussolini in 1923. [14] In the mid-1930s
Crowley befriended another seminal intellectual of the

---

[14] See chapters 52-57 in *Gargantua* by Francois Rabelais, for the
description of the Abbey of Theleme, the real source of the OTO's
"new religion."

20th century, Aldous Huxley, author of *Brave New World* and one of the first pioneers of psychedelic hallucinogens in California in the 1950s. Huxley was a descendant of Thomas Huxley, an early proponent of Darwin's theory of evolution who coined the term "agnostic" as a description of his personal non-creed. After Crowley's death in 1947 the OTO advanced rapidly within the corridors of popular culture.

In the Sixties, Crowley's hour had arrived. The Beatles, as noted earlier, included him on the over of their album, and Led Zeppelin's rock-star guitarist Jimmy Page purchased Crowley's mansion in Boleskine, Scotland, overlooking the home of the fabled Loch Ness "Monster." Page agreed to collaborate with Crowley's Hollywood disciple, the appropriately-named Kenneth Anger, on the soundtrack of Anger's cult-film, "Lucifer Rising" starring Charles Manson's associate, Bobby Beausoliel, who would later be convicted of the murder of musician Gary Hinman.

In Virgin Megastores, a paperback of Crowley's book, *Confessions* is a virtual chart-topper. A CD of Crowley wailing "Enochian Calls" and reading his own poetry (about himself—"Bury me in a nameless grave; I came from God the world to save"), sells like *haunt* cakes. Major bookstores carry a dozen of his works. It is simply a fact that the advent of Harry Potter would have been impossible without the Beast as a forerunner. As one teenager told me (who, in a burst of heartfelt enthusiasm, gave me a copy of Crowley's book, *Diary of a Drug Fiend,* like an evangelist passing out a Gideon Bible), "He has a great deal he can teach us."

But more important than the triumph of the OTO's Aleister Crowley in pop culture, is the advance of Crowleyanity in mainstream culture. C. S. Lewis, the popular Christian author, called our time a "post-Christian" age. But Crowley had predicted it: the "Aeon of Horus," the age of the Crowned and Conquering Child, said Crowley, must come, overthrowing the "Aeon of Osiris," the age of the Dying God. The New Age announced by Crowley is one in which God the Father is thrown off by Horus the Child, a rebellious and developing youth culture, reckless and dangerous, but, from Crowley's viewpoint—essential to evolution and control--since the OTO-led Left-wing rebellion would spark an OTO-led Right-wing reaction.

The doublespeak of Crowley and his successors is staggering. These diabolists are leaders of boomerang movements which have enslaved the hypnotized seekers into an Orwellian acceptance of conditions which are the opposite to those they advocate and foretell. As a result, the herd imagines it is advancing even while it embraces the skeleton like a 33rd Degree Mason during an initiation. The parallel between the OTO initiate and the American populace is remarkable. Both have been or are presently being conditioned and when the time is right, they will welcome a leader who will allow them the "quiet wisdom of the cattle," which they will have truly become. Is not the Aeon of Horus upon us?

IV

Wiccan Witches and Magical Masons

"Enough of Because! Be he damned for a dog!"

The last chapter ended with a bald assertion that the Aeon of Horus is upon us and one sign of that is the ubiquitous presence of "Wicca" or "good witchcraft" in our contemporary popular culture. Books, movies and websites on this topic are all the rage. Wicca forms its own organizational matrix in a society hungry for alternatives to the sterility of the Establishment. The only problem is, Wicca *is* the Establishment, at least a wing of it.

There are vast sections in bookstores reserved for "Magickal" studies (note the OTO spelling of the word), volumes about the goddess, tables of "Teen Witch Kits," and scads of other books of rituals, amulets and similar occult feminism.

But what passes for "Wicca" is a hoax on the public perpetrated by none other than the OTO. Wicca is not traditional witchcraft, as any traditional witch will be quick to declare. Traditional witchcraft has no "Wiccan Rede," partially composed by Aleister Crowley, with its modification of his Law of Thelema: "An' it harm none, do what ye will."

While Wiccans readily give great credit to Gerald Gardner for his role in "reviving" Wicca, they choose to distance themselves from anything that smacks of Satan worship or Crowleyanity. But here's the dirty little secret most Wiccans won't admit: Freemason and OTO initiate Gerald Gardner and his Freemasonic brother and OTO superior Aleister Crowley created *the entire system* of Wicca. The Three Degrees were stolen from Freemasonry, as were the Five Points of Fellowship (given, however, an altogether new and creative interpretation via the OTO). Wiccans traditionally stand "sky clad" (naked), and their culminating ritual is a "transfer of power" through OTO-style sex magick. Such is the Wicca concocted by Gardner and Crowley: This is paganism in a broad sense, but nonetheless shaped into an OTO/Freemasonic magic mold and dispensed like candy. [1]

Wicca has admittedly evolved, branching out, dropping the lodge structure and claiming to be the authentic, repressed current of ancient goddess-worship throughout the centuries. If only Wiccans knew that their supposed "ancient" feminist religion is of a far more recent patrimony/patriarchy, concocted by two goat-like male masonic wizards.

Harry Potter and Hollywood

Gardner's marketing skills were impressive. Crowley always lacked the popular touch, being too erudite. Gardner could package sex magick to sell, and did so. Today, Wicca is booming. The Harry Potter genre is a multimillion dollar cinematic and publishing phenomenon. Shortly after the first Potter film was released, Jess Wynn, spokesman for the Pagan Federation of England offered thanks to the Harry Potter books because in its wake, his organization received thousands of inquiries from teenagers seeking information about "The Craft," (a popular code-word for witchcraft). In the meantime, Pope John Paul II got in on the act, bestowing his blessing on Harry Potter, while liberal Protestants have published books purporting to prove that the "Gospel" is somehow contained in the occult and alchemical world of Hogwarts.

Under Michael Eisner, The Walt Disney Co. (which has seen Walt's surviving nephew, Roy E. Disney, part ways with Eisner in disgust), has become one of the mass initiators of children through visual processing loaded with brazen occult themes. As one example, the animated film "Atlantis" contains a surfeit of OTO symbolism. The cartoon character "Scooby Doo" has also been transformed into an evangelist for Witchcraft. In "Scooby Doo and the Witch's Ghost," kids learn that one Sarah Ravencroft, burned long ago in a Puritan village, was really a "Wiccan," and that "Wiccans were people who were in tune with the forces of nature and used them for healing purposes."

---

[1] Cf. Allen Greenfield, "The Secret History of Modern Witchcraft," in Richard Metzger, *Book of Lies: Disinformation Guide to Magick and the Occult.*

The only other book of late to rival Harry Potter as pop-cult literary *wunderkind* is the pagan goddess-advocacy of *The Da Vinci Code*, by Dan Brown, which for more than 75 weeks was at the top of the *New York Times* bestseller list. "The pendulum is swinging," says Brown's imaginary protagonist from Harvard University. "We are beginning to sense the need to restore the sacred feminine." Indeed, and her name is the Great Whore, "Babalon" as personified by a stream of modern pop stars from Britney to Madonna, all glimmering with the OTO's Luciferian morning-stardust and Kabbalah strings, exactly as Crowley wished. There are numerous other books and movies of this type, together with pentagrams worn around the neck, pantacles on the desk at work, "stress" or "ritual consultants" for corporations who light a candle and lead the confused employees through some watered-down Wicca—such events are commonplace today. Even many modern Catholic nuns have adopted these practices, substituting the Wiccan greeting "Blessed be" for the old Catholic "Ave Maria." Popular TV shows like "Sabrina" and "Charmed" push Wicca down the throats of young children. Nobody knows, and nobody cares. If little Johnny goes from Harry Potter to Aleister Crowley, it's probably "just a phase..."

Freemasonry: The Inner Secrets

Wicca is not the only "Craft." Freemasonry also calls itself the Craft. By combining the two, Crowley and Gardner made a blend as natural as a Caffé Mocha. Frequently, however, Crowley is trotted out and denounced in some Masonic article; the OTO is deemed "irregular" — the ultimate Masonic slur on a lodge, somewhat parallel to "heretical" — and all claims of Luciferian tomfoolery in the lodges are laughed off as old hoaxes. This dodge runs completely counter to the OTO's version of itself, since it holds itself to be the essence of Freemasonry. But the "official" tension between the OTO and the run-of-the-mill Masonic lodge is recognized by Thelemites. As one of their top leaders told this writer, "To Masons, we're witches, and to witches, we're Masons."

Although I played along with his statement, I know that Wiccans are essentially naked Freemasons, so while he probably thought his little jest was pitched over my head, I caught it and mentally tagged him out.

Now it is time to bring to any Freemasonic readers the very thing they swear to seek — Light. For there is probably no group of men more in the dark than those miserable souls who undertake such a search in a Blue Lodge.

They are told that Freemasonry is not a religion; that it is not dogmatic, and has no fixed beliefs; that it is not a "secret society", but a "society with secrets;" that it requires a mere belief in God, being open to all men of good will; that it is a system of morality which utilizes the symbols of masonry to teach ethical lessons through ritual; that it is compatible with all religions and beliefs; that it is a benevolent, charitable, fraternal service-club.

"Blue Lodge" and Scottish Rite Masonry

Let us simplify the task of initiation immensely, rending the veil and ushering in the light of reality. To do so, we will have recourse to the words of the most famous leaders in the history of Freemasonry, Albert Mackey and Albert Pike.

Mackey is the author of the pile of verbiage in the front of most masonic Bibles called "Questions and Answers, One Hundred and Sixty Questions and Answers...Pertaining to the Symbolism of Masonry and its Connection with the Bible." Mackey became grand secretary of the Grand Lodge, grand high priest of the Grand Chapter, grand master of the Grand Council, and general grand high priest of the General Grand Chapter of the United States. He was secretary general of the Supreme Council of the 33rd Degree, and the prolific author of foundational Masonic works such as *A Lexicon of Freemasonry*, the *Encyclopedia of Freemasonry*, and *The History of Freemasonry*.

One finds Mackey repeating over and over that the first three degrees are all that an initiate need to be a Mason. But Mackey did not heed his own counsel: he was simultaneously a leader in the Grand "Blue" Lodge (three degree system) and the Scottish Rite Lodge (thirty-three degree system). All Blue Lodge Masons should wonder: Why did Brother Mackey bother with the upper degrees at all, becoming a leader within that system?

Mackey explains: "They [the three degrees] were the *text*, and the high degrees (are) the *commentary*" (emphasis supplied). In other words, every secret in Freemasonry is really contained in the ritual of the third degree, but no Mason typically understands that ritual (if ever), until he is initiated into the Scottish Rite.

The esteemed Freemason, the Reverend George Oliver, encapsulates this dilemma in this bizarre statement in his *Dictionary of Symbolical Masonry*, "...the light of a Master Mason is darkness visible."

Pike's Momentous "Revelation of the Method"

Regarding the higher degrees, no authority exceeds Albert Pike, Sovereign Grand Commander of the Southern Jurisdiction of Scottish Rite Masonry (the world's most powerful masonic body) from 1859 until his death in 1891. Pike rewrote every Scottish Rite ritual, creating the 20th century system that remains in force as of this writing. His massive tome *Morals and Dogma* was distributed to every Scottish Rite "adept." The following quote from Pike will help to elucidate: 1. the extent to which most third degree Master Masons are intentionally deceived and deliberately left in the dark, a "darkness" that is not only "visible" to their dishonest lodge masters (the "adepts"), it is imposed by them; and 2. the undeniable Luciferian nature of Freemasonry. [2]

Here is Pike's self-confessed manifesto of mendacity:

"The Blue Degrees are but the outer court or portico of the Temple. Part of the symbols are displayed there to the Initiate, but he is intentionally misled by false interpretations. It is not intended that he shall understand them; but it is intended that he shall imagine he understands them. Their true explication is reserved for the Adepts, the Princes of Masonry...It is well enough for the mass of those called Masons, to imagine that all is contained in the Blue Degrees; and who so attempts to undeceive them will labor in vain, and without any true reward violate his obligations as an Adept....

---

[2] Albert Pike, *Morals and Dogma of the Ancient and Accepted Scottish Rite of Freemasonry*.(1871). Reprinted Washington, D.C: House of the Temple, 1966. Cf. pp. 819; 104-105; 839; 321; 817.

Masonry...conceals its secrets from all except the Adepts and Sages, or the Elect, and uses false explanations and misinterpretations of its symbols to mislead those who deserve only to be misled; to conceal the Truth, which it calls Light, from them, and to draw them away from it...."

Pike here reveals the secret identity of the masonic god and the true nature of the popes and kings who will ascend "altar-and-throne" in his prophesied masonic-dominated future (keep in mind he was writing in 1871):

"The Occult Science of the Ancient Magi was concealed under the shadows of the Ancient Mysteries: it was imperfectly revealed or rather disfigured by the Gnostics: it is guessed at under the obscurities that cover the pretended crimes of the Templars; and it is found enveloped in enigmas that seem impenetrable, in the Rites of the Highest Masonry....LUCIFER, the Light-bearer! Strange and mysterious name to give to the Spirit of Darkness! Lucifer, the Son of the Morning! Is it he who bears the Light...? Doubt it not!....the World will soon come to us for its Sovereigns and Pontiffs. We shall constitute the equilibrium of the Universe, and be rulers over the Masters of the World."

Modern masons try to perform damage control concerning this undeniable evidence of masonic Luciferianism by claiming that a. relatively few Masons ever bothered to read *Morals and Dogma* and were not influenced by it; or b. it is not authoritative because Pike was "only" the head of the Scottish Rite, Southern Jurisdiction (encompassing thirty-five states, a half-million masons and 20% of the total masonic membership of the U.S.). Knowing the extent to which Pike and his elite brethren chortled about keeping even other Masons in the Blue Lodge deceived, it should not be difficult to perceive that the public at large is considered fair game for the "hoodwink." [3]

In this case, what the Lodge boys have "forgotten" to tell us in their scramble to defuse Pike's brazen Luciferian revelation, is that the Scottish Rite of Masonry, Southern Jurisdiction was the most powerful in the world. Hence,

---

[3] "Hoodwink" is a masonic code word for deception. Candidates prepared for initiation in the Lodge are blindfolded or "hoodwinked" prior to the ritual.

Pike's monumental *Morals and Dogma* was, as its title presaged, the defining dogmatic statement of Masonic belief.

Pike's declaration demonstrates the nature of their liar's institute: a system of symbols, which, in the first three degrees are explained as "moral lessons" and other such sop until the candidate is deemed worthy to learn the true occult explanations, if indeed he is ever judged worthy. Only then will he find that the light that he has pledged to seek must be consciously received from Lucifer, the "Light-Bearer."

Only then will the Mason understand that the Lodge serves the staggering ambition of the Cryptocracy for building true world domination, as symbolized in the masonic third degree ceremony centered on the interruption of the building of the Temple of Solomon, which Hiram Abiff leaves unfinished — supposedly so that the Freemasons of our era will complete it (the same message of a clandestine task left undone is conveyed by the unfinished pyramid on the Great Seal of the United States, as shown on the one dollar bill). [4]

Freemasonry is a nursery of Luciferianism from which promising candidates are selected, while others are left forever in the dark, content to exploit their good-old-boy connections, play their charity charade and exchange arcane hand signals with judges, lawyers and jurors for mutual benefit of the guilty.

Aleister Crowley informed the Brotherhood that the serpent in the Garden of Eden is the savior of mankind: "This serpent, SATAN, is not the enemy of Man, but He who made Gods of our race, knowing Good and Evil; He bade 'Know Thyself!' and taught Initiation." [5]

Masonic diabolism again came to the fore in 1917, during the bicentennial celebration of the official birth of

---

[4] In the third degree, the blindfolded candidate, as "Hiram Abiff," is unexpectedly "slain" (struck with a mallet on the forehead) and "resurrected," leaving the Temple of Solomon unfinished.

[5] Aleister Crowley with Mary Desti and Leila Waddell, *Magick: Liber ABA*, Book 4, Parts I-IV. (York Beach: Samuel Weiser, 1997).

Grand Lodge Freemasonry, when Grand Orient Freemasons in Italy marched in Vatican City with black banners depicting the Archangel Michael being trodden underfoot by Satan, a reversal of the traditional Christian image of St. Michael trampling the devil. [6]

Luciferianism Decoded

Freemason Albert Lantoine, 33° wrote a book in 1937 addressed to the Pope in which he said, "Possessing critical and inquisitive minds, we are the servants of Satan. You, the guardians of truth, are the servants of God. These two complement one another. Each needs the other." [7]

Interestingly, he later corrected himself and said that he did not use "quite the correct term" and should have said "servants of Lucifer." The distinction may be lost on some.

The name Lucifer is derived from Jerome's Latin Vulgate translation of Isaiah 14:12: "*Quomodo cecidisti de caelo, Lucifer, qui mane oriebaris?*" (How art thou fallen from heaven thou Lucifer, son of the morning?) Patristic tradition taught that Satan had another name before his fall, which the Church Fathers denominated as "Light bearer," and which Jerome rendered into Latin literally, as "Lucifer" (*luc/lux* ([light] + *fer* [bearing). In the original Hebrew he is called the "shining one," to whom Nebuchadnezzar and all other tyrannical kings of the earth who are idolatrously worshipped, are compared. Therefore, the masonic identification with Lucifer is an attempt to invoke the supernatural force that energizes tyrannical rule. (For an allusion to Lucifer as Satan, see

---

[6] Maximilian Kolbe, a Polish seminarian pursuing his studies in Rome, witnessed this demonic spectacle and was so deeply disturbed by it that after his ordination, he formed one of the largest and most militant anti-masonic and anti-rabbinic media networks in the Catholic world, the "Militia of the Immaculata". Imprisoned in Auschwitz as a Polish nationalist, he is alleged to have died of lethal injection there in 1941. He was canonized in 1982.

[7] Albert Lantoine, *Lettre au Souverain Pontife*. Cited by Vicomte Leon de Poncins, Freemasonry and the Vatican (Palmdale, Calif.: Omni/Christian Book Club, 1968), p.11.

Jesus' statement in Luke 10:18). The severe scriptural animadversion to the perfection and glories of Lucifer/Satan as celebrated by Freemasons and the OTO, can be found in Ezekiel 28:12-15, while verses 16-19 combine characteristics of Satan and a tyrannical king who is energized by Satanic characteristics, in the same way that Isaiah 14 connotes both Lucifer and the kings of Babylon who pattern their reign after him

Thelema Implants the Double Mind

Freemasons and OTO Crowleyites, in their "moderate/progressive" Left-wing disguise, pose as enlightened alternatives to the "darkness, superstition and horrors" attributed, with the song-song monotony of the playground, to the "Catholic Church and the Inquisition." They say this even as they state their own intention to lie to their patsies in the Blue Lodge and farm human beings for their "mutton and wool," in a future tyranny and a new inquisition that makes the Church version look like a respite at Sunnybrook Farm.

Catholic scholar Thomas Molnar traces the command process of the Abbey of Thelema to the terror of the French Revolution and the Gulag of Soviet Communism, both iron-fisted systems having been imposed in the name of lofty masonic ideals of fraternity and equality, and Judeo-Bolshevik promises of paradise for workers and peasants. Molnar makes reference to the *utopian* or heaven-on-earth conceit of these totalitarian systems, which peddle the perfection of man and the kabbalistic aspiration to repair God's supposedly defective creation, through the intervention (and appeal to) human brain power and other god-like powers of the occult superman/sorcerer. Ellen Myers, expanding on Molnar, writes: "Utopians demand absolute perfection and purity in society, a seemingly attractive trait until we realize that their goal and 'perhaps [their] main motivation' is an unnatural, anti-human perfection and purity *of their own invention*...Molnar perceptively points out that utopian perfectionism in general 'is actually a conscious and concentrated form of *self-divinization*" which leads in reality, to hell on earth-- to the guillotine and the gulag. [8]

These movements, pitched to the public in the name of an alternative to Churchianity and Dogma are, in their practice and implementation, Satanic, for who else desires hell on earth but Satan, and who else has the mocking cunning to achieve such an infernal objective in the name of heaven on earth? Who is the father of lies and of the double-mind that entertains those lies without being troubled by the insanity of simultaneously countenancing diametrically opposed opposites?

Yet Satan is the Arthur C. Clarke "Overlord" we encounter *only in the Cryptocracy's last act,* at the terminus of Horus' brief lifespan -- "Childhood's End." The occult sales pitch to the conceited modern mentality begins first with the illumination and "luhv" of the more attractive and soothing figure of the light-bearing Lucifer, herald of a New Order of the Ages, or "Golden Dawn."

Exemplifying kabbalistic contradiction, the merging of the two opposing pillars of Rabbi Isaac Luria's initiatory icon, the kabbalistic Tree of Life, or the integrating of the two male and female aspects of divinity in the kabbalistic scripture the Zohar, Freemason/OTO adepts excel in generating a hypnosis of confusing but convincing double-talk. A personification of this occult split-personality syndrome is Arthur Edward Waite, who, in his *New Encyclopedia of Freemasonry,* scoffs at the facts about Lucifer and Freemasonry as so much nonsense, while including an illustration featuring "Lucifer, emerging from clouds." Waite is also the author of *The Book of Black Magic and Pacts,* the very book which inspired Aleister Crowley to join the Golden Dawn, of which Waite was a member. [9]

John Robinson, after writing an acclaimed account of Freemasonry, *Born in Blood*, went on to become a Mason himself. In his work of Masonic apologetics, *A Pilgrim's Path*, Robinson's double mind tries to reconcile the

---

[8] Cf. Ellen Myers, "Thomas Molnar," at: http://www.creationism.org/csshs/v10n2p13.htm (emphasis supplied).

[9] The Hermetic Order of the Golden Dawn derived its name from Lucifer. Cf. Israel Regardie, *The Golden Dawn,* pp. 290-91, 298.

Scottish Rite's Luciferianism and ends up descending to insane absurdity: "Pike and company did not refer to an evil spirit, but simply the Bearer of Light or Education." In a similar vein, British OTO leader Kenneth Grant writes in *The Magickal Revival* that the associations of Crowley with "black magic" are nothing but an "ill-considered calumny." But a few sentences later Grant states that in more innocent pagan times, "Crowley's Cult of Satan...would have evoked no feelings of perversity and guilt" (!)

What does the OTO regard as black evil? Who are the "Black Brothers" denounced by Crowley? From the Kabbalist-Masonic perspective, the foul demons are the tiny remnant of *authentic* Christians (as opposed to the mass of pseudo Christians --actually "Judeo-Churchians"-- who have an "appearance of Godliness" and "Jesus Jesus Jesus" on their lips, while serving the neo-con wing of the Cryptocracy). In the Instruction for the OTO's Eighth Degree, Christ's *true ecclesia* is defined as comprising the "foul demon of the Christians."

The OTO calls anyone a "Black Brother" who did not have the spiritual daring or psychological toughness to "cross the Abyss" into cognate OTO groups and affiliates, due to some vestige of conscience regarded as hopelessly un-Thelemic.

In spite of sophistry and rationalizations of Freemasonry's diabolic orientation, truly initiated Freemasonry — even in a mainstream version such as the Scottish Rite — culminates in an embrace of Lucifer as teacher and the serpent of Genesis as Savior.

What then of Wicca? Of Masonry? Of the melding of both by the OTO? Is the OTO truly "witchcraft to Masons, and Masonry to witches?"

By melding a modern witch-Craft and a modern lodge-Craft, the OTO has actually only played a variation of a tune common to both -- the pipes of Pan, the kabbalistic dance of the goat of the Sabbat, the siren-song of the one so hotly denied after the heralding of the golden dawn, but so secretly adored in the gnostic night -- before the cock crows.

V

The Palladium

"Behold! The rituals of the old time are black."

Writing about the Cult of the Beast and connecting it with Freemasonry is sure to arouse one indignant reply in particular from the Masons and their stooges.

The reply is predictable, because it is a staple of Masonic propaganda. Sooner or later the Freemason is bound to bring up George Washington, and the righteous, patriotic indignation will take on something close to the following tone:

"Are you going to cast aspersions on George Washington himself, and the Founding Fathers of this land, by calling into disrepute their own Brotherhood from whence they derived their very notions of liberty?"

Contrary to this delusional brag, the Masons' favorite poster boy George Washington joined the Lodge in his youth and abandoned it upon gaining a few years and a bit of commensurate wisdom. After playing the Lodge game and receiving his Third Degree in 1753 at Fredericksburg, Virginia, he quit. He wrote in 1798:

"I have little more to add than thanks for your wishes, and favorable sentiments, *except to correct an error you have run into of my presiding over the English lodges in this country. The fact is I preside over none, nor have I been in one more than once or twice within the last thirty years.* I believe, notwithstanding, that none of the lodges in this country are contaminated with the principles ascribed to the society of the Illuminati." (Emphasis supplied). [1]

In this statement Washington shows that he has consciously distanced himself from Freemasonry, hardly the "poster boy" the Masons paint him to be.

---

[1] George Washington, Letter dated Mt. Vernon, September 25, 1798, cited in *The Character, Claims and Practical Workings of Freemasonry* by Charles G. Finney, 1869 (Tyler, Texas: JKI Publishing, 1998). p. 150.

Washington, Jefferson and Franklin

At the same time, Washington was hopeful that the overtly diabolical Illuminati which he had read about in John Robison's *Proofs of a Conspiracy* (1798), had not spread *within the Lodges* of the New World. This view of his, which we now know was in error, was relflected in part by the errors that Robison himself makes in minimizing the connection between the Illuminati and British Freemasonry in his book. That these errors were afoot in America as a whole, as documented by the eminent Congregationalist preacher Rev. Jedidiah Morse and others, Washington did not deny. He condemned the "diabolical tenets" of the Illuminati while acknowledging with alarm that their doctrines had in fact spread in the United States. In 1798 he wrote that "no one is more truly satisfied of this fact than I am..."

Founding Father Thomas Jefferson derived many political points from the Catholic Cardinal Robert Bellarmine, who vigorously opposed the absolute monarchism of the Anglican Church and its doctrine of the "divine right of kings" as promulgated by King James I. [2]

In spite of the claim that the United States was begun as a "Masonic plot," the truth is that most Masons by far were Loyalists who fought for the Crown, a masonic institution which by that time was dripping in occultism and entrenched in Lodge control.

The misprision frequently arises when a naive conspiracy researcher skims a few books written by the Masons themselves and begins to believe what he reads, or stumbles through a Masonic Temple tour and swallows the swill in the pamphlets and pictures. Such individuals might with equal justification believe a Mormon Temple history tour about the "forgotten appearance of Jesus" to the Indians as Quetzlcoatl, the feathered serpent. Prudent readers should keep in mind that Freemasons are like the old Soviets in their historical claims: just as the Soviets

---

[2] Cf. Alfred ORahilly, "Catholic Origin of Democracy," *Studies*, March, 1919 and *The Political Philosophy of St. Robert Bellarmine* by Rev. Fr. John Clement Rager, (Spokane, Washington, 1995) p. 84.

were fond of claiming many great historical geniuses as
"one of them," so the Masons like to claim an absurdly long
list of great men. If you can believe the Freemasons,
everyone who benefited mankind was in the lodge—and
who knows, maybe your wife goes to the Order of the
Eastern Star when she says she is at the mall, or your
husband when he "works late?"

But does not common sense tell us that such claims are
cheap? Proof is the test of an historian. Rather than
rebounding from modern Masonic America and
denigrating everything in toto about America from the
Mayflower forward, disaffected men should take a page
from Missourians in dealing with Masons and their claims
and say, "show me." Knowledgeable historians of
Freemasonry realize that deception and trickery abound
when it comes to writings produced by a masonic lodge,
which are as trustworthy as old *Pravda* tales about the
Communists of Russia.

Some researchers may well be promoting lodge
disinformation deliberately. The pro-Masonic view of our
nation's history has actually spread from Manly Palmer
Hall to traditional Catholic circles. Confused but convinced
Catholics are running around repeating the boasts of the
Lodge concerning their alleged role in the American
Revolution and seeing the procession of American history
as one large masonic unfolding in every detail. Part of the
error may be excusable to the extent that modern America
has been alchemically processed, thanks to the OTO, to a
Crowleyized level in which it has lived down to the
Ayatollah Khomeini's 1980's description of the United
States as "The Great Satan." Yet historians must honor
truth, and connecting a modern America which would
have repulsed George Washington with the man himself is
as unfair as claiming that the unscriptural distortions that
crept into the Catholic Church following Rome's Second
Vatican Council are the fault of St. Paul and St. Peter, or
that Emerson's Unitarian creed is the direct product of the
writings of Puritan Jonathan Edwards. History has to
draw certain lines and call fouls, out of fairness and
respect for scrupulosity and exactitude, the building blocks
of truth.

What, then, is the truth about the men who fought the War of Independence? Like any group, the herd of men which attacked their British oppressors were bound to contain a black sheep or two. The prize in this case must go to Benjamin Franklin, who in a few respects was a good forerunner to Crowley, although this side of Franklin is little known. Benjamin Franklin was a member of the Hell Fire Club, an eighteenth-century Satanic society associated with Sir Francis Dashwood, whose members met in an abandoned abbey at Medmenham on the Thames. As occult chronicler Montague Summers writes in *Witchcraft and Black Magic*, pp. 220-21: "That the visitors to Medmenham, and indeed many members of this infamous Society, were lecherous rakehells who assembled for the practice of unbridled lewdness is of course, a fact beyond question, but it is also certain that among the vile there were viler still, 'the elect', or in plain words Satanists, devoted to the worship of the fiend."

Daniel Mannix noted in a later history: "A solemn toast was drunk to the powers of darkness. A deep-toned gong was struck and the procession marched into the chapel. Some time before, Dashwood had obtained a book on black magic from the bookseller Edmund Curll, who had a publishing house in Covent Gardens where he printed pornographic works for a select coterie. Dashwood was one of his best customers. At his patron's request, Curll obtained for him a treatise on occultism, probably a copy of 'The Key of Solomon' or the 'Kabala.' At that time, books on occultism were illegal and considered in the same class as pornography, and only illicit publishers handled them. This book, whatever it was, was the basis for the club's magical ceremonies." [3]

Jefferson's Christianity was certainly peculiar to the intellectual ferment of the Protestant America of that time. Jefferson's major concern with traditional Christianity was its tendency to lapse into a tyrannical and avaricious priestcraft, a concern as old *Piers the Ploughman* and Geoffrey Chaucer's "The Pardoner's Tale." His *Jefferson Bible* omitted most of Christ's miracles

---

[3] Daniel P. Mannix, *The Hellfire Club* (New York: ibooks, 2001) pp. 31-32.

because Jefferson sincerely believed they had been added by later writers in order to detract from the brilliant simplicity of Jesus' noble ethics.

So how do we respond to the Freemasons with their posters of George Washington in a lodge apron? Can we really link George Washington to the likes of Aleister Crowley? But the question is nonsense. The succinct reply is this: that some of the Founding Fathers, caught up in a little-understood and fairly new fad (Freemasonry had only pushed itself into view in 1717), became Freemasons. But these Masons were typically not highly initiated (Washington only reached the third degree). Many were still undoubtedly abiding in the "outer portico of the Temple." Ben Franklin seems to be the only one who enjoyed wallowing in the Inner Squalor.

The ignorance of any lodge dupes aside--who lend their good name (if they have one) to the entire spectrum of Freemasonry—it is incontestable that the lodge retains its Inner Squalor for the privileged elites. Aleister Crowley and his OTO Beast Cult is simply a crystallizing of that kabbalistic sanctum of blood and depravity. If the "bad name" of the "Wickedest Man in the World" negates their "good name" by the connection, they cannot solve the problem by denying the connection. They must admit the facts and decide if the facts disturb them or not. Ironically, they have an excellent example to follow: George Washington. If they wish to take his lead, they should, like him, quit the Lodge. In the case of most Freemasons, however, I will wager that their lodge-enhanced career track washes aside these concerns.

The preceding history lesson inspires a fair question: when were Masons initiated into a deeper level of understanding, into something like Ben Franklin's Hell Fire Club, or an Illuminati Lodge? Where was the "inner sanctum Freemasonry" traditionally disclosed to the ultra elite?

Diana Vaughan
Priestess of Lucifer and the Palladium

To answer that question we must consult a labyrinthine collection of hotly contested books from France which began to surface approximately one hundred years ago, under the patronage of Gabriel Jogand-Pagés, who wrote under the nom de plume, "Leo Taxil." His works purported to divulge a great secret and to reveal the system behind the Scottish Rite of Freemasonry's highly guarded inner sanctum; the peak of its inner circle, Albert Pike's Satanic "Palladium" masonry. These books sparked an uproar, since they testified to Pike's leadership of a Satanic religion. But at the peak of the furor, Leo Taxil suddenly and inexplicably vigorously denounced his own work as a hoax. As a result, a great deal of subsequent exposure of Freemasonry was forever condemned as a replay of the "Taxil fraud."

But was it all a hoax? Here is where we enter a veritable onion skin where the mind that cannot peel layer after layer of guile will be left bewildered and demoralized. In truth the Taxil revelations are more complex and are not easily resolved with simplistic explanations.

Masons claim that Taxil was simply a disgruntled, expelled Entered Apprentice (First Degree) Mason who turned on them for base motives. If that is the case, how did Taxil manage to publish accurate details from numerous advanced secret rituals in the higher degrees? This writer can attest to this truth because I possess in my personal archive both Taxil's original descriptions and the actual secret rituals themselves. How would a sour-grapes low-level, ex-Mason have gained these explosive secrets?

Taxil stated that Pike's Palladium rite contained the degrees "Companion of Ulysses" and "Companion of Penelope," and that the lodges were "a slop barrel, a shameful and hidden plague, a devouring rottenness formed and supplied by the most infamous vices," in other words, a fount of ritual sex magic. He called these "Androgynous Lodges" (lodges containing women) "a harem." Here we have a particular point for which Taxil was ridiculed in the media of the day, since "sex magick" was inconceivable in that era, except as the province of the most degenerate and abandoned segments of the lower "criminal class"; hardly something that would be advocated by men of esteemed social status and public repute.

Moreover, did not Taxil confess that his Palladium

revelations were a lurid hoax? Yet the respected Masonic historian Robert Macoy, 33° included the "Order of the Palladium" in his authoritative Dictionary. Macoy wrote that "the rules admitted both sexes to membership...The male members were called the 'Companions of Ulysses,' and the female the 'Sisters of Penelope.' The seal of the order was a heart, crowned with flowers, upon an altar, ornamented with a garland, with a branch of laurel at the right, and another of palm, at the left. Upon the heart was the inscription: *"Je sais aimer"* (I know how to love). This device and the intimacy which prevailed between the Companions of Ulysses and the Sisters of Penelope indicate with sufficient plainness the certain end and principal object of the order of the Palladium." Macoy is here alluding to ceremonies with more than a passing resemblance to the sexual rites which were the axis of the the "higher, inner sanctum" OTO Freemasonry of the 20th century.

Even Freemason and Golden Dawn leader A. E. Waite, who helped to lead the charge against the Taxil literature, admitted that the Order of the Palladium existed, but downplayed its significance. Yet its essence, *magica sexualis,* was anything but insignificant, as Waite well knew, writing elsewhere of the "Garden of Venus" and the "Mystery of Sex," as that "act of love on the spiritual as on the physical plane (which) has its fruition in an ejaculation..." [4]

Waite devotes over 27 pages to the subject of the "mystery of sex" in his work *The Holy Kabbalah*, deeming sex central to Kabbalism. Waite also refers in this same book to Albert Pike: "No person who is acquainted with *Morals and Dogma* can fail to trace the hand of the occultist therein, and it is to be observed that, passing from Grade to Grade in the direction of the highest, this instruction becomes more and more Kabbalistic." [5]

Waite attempts try to "clear" Pike of Palladium charges but extols Pike's occultism; he minimizes sex magic in the

---

[4] Arthur Edward Waite, *A New Encyclopedia of Freemasonry*, I, 302-303.

[5] Waite, *The Holy Kabbalah*, p. 553.

masonic Palladium as an isolated, minor event of a minor order, yet speaks of this "mystery" as central to the Kabbalah, and therefore central to Pike's advanced Freemasonry. Discerning readers will spot Waite's guile.

Montague Summers writes of the discovery of the Palladium Temple: "In May, 1895, when the legal representatives of the Borghese family visited the Palazzo Borghese, which had been rented for some time in separate floors or suites, they found some difficulty in obtaining admission to certain apartments on the first floor, the occupant of which seemed unaware that the lease was about to expire. By virtue of the terms of the agreement, however, he was obliged to allow them to inspect the premises to see if any structural repairs or alterations were necessary, as Prince Scipione Borghese, who was about to be married, intended immediately to take up his residence in the ancestral home with his bride. One door the tenant obstinately refused to unlock, and when pressed he betrayed the greatest confusion. The agents finally pointed out that they were within their rights to employ actual force...

"When the keys had been produced, the cause of the reluctance was soon plain. The room within was inscribed with the words *Templum Palladicum*. The walls were hung all round from ceiling to floor with heavy curtains of silk damask, scarlet and black, excluding the light; at the further end there stretched a large tapestry upon which was woven in more than life-size a figure of Lucifer, colossal, triumphant, dominating the whole. Exactly beneath an altar had been built, amply furnished for the liturgy of hell: candles, vessels, rituals, missal, nothing was lacking. Cushioned prie-dieus and luxurious chairs, crimson and gold, were set in order for the assistants; the chamber being lit by electricity, fantastically arrayed so as to glare from an enormous human eye. The visitors soon quitted the accursed spot, the scene of devil-worship and blasphemy, nor had they any desire more nearly to examine the appointments of this infernal chapel." [6]

A modern writer, William Schnoebelen (formerly OTO, IX°) stated that he was inducted into a Palladium Lodge (Resurrection #13), in Chicago in the late 1970s. Schnoebelen was allegedly initiated by David DePaul, associate of Michael "Aquarius" Bertiaux, in turn a close associate of Kenneth Grant. According to Michael Bertiaux, a leader of the OTOA—*Ordo Templi Orientis Antiqua* (a cognate OTO group), DePaul restarted the Palladium after supposedly invoking the spirit of Diana Vaughan. If Taxil was a hoaxer then this invocation is difficult to understand since "Diana Vaughan" had been "Priestess of Lucifer" in the Freemasonic Palladium rite described by Taxil. If Vaughan was a figment of Taxil's fevered imagination why would she be invoked by an OTO faction in the 1970s?

Another anomaly: the Palladium rite oath is the same as that given in 1908 by former Freemason Monsieur Copin Albancelli: *"Gloire et Amour à Lucifer! Haine! haine! haine! Au Dieu maudit! maudit! maudit!"* ("Glory and Love for Lucifer! Hatred! Hatred! Hatred! To God accursed, accursed, accursed!"). Albancelli wrote: "It is professed in these societies that all that the Christian God commands is disagreeable to Lucifer; that all that He forbids is, on the contrary, agreeable to Lucifer; that in consequence one must do all that the Christian God forbids and that one must shun like fire all that He commands. I repeat that with regard to all that, I have the proofs under my hand. I have read and studied hundreds of documents relating to one of these societies, documents that I have not permission to publish and which emanate from the members, men and women, of the group in question."

Occult sources indicate that Albert Pike was chartered

---

[6] Montague Summers, *The History of Witchcraft* (New York: Barnes & Noble Books, 1993) p. 152-53. The reference given by Summers is Maggio, *Corriere Nazionale di Torino*, 1895, although it is uncertain if this account borrowed from an associate of Taxil or vice-versa, given the similarities. It is included as corroborating information, absent strict proof of plagiarism.

to run a branch of the *Societas Rosicruciana* in the US, a Rosicrucian Order which intersected with both the OTO and the Hermetic Brotherhood of Luxor (Light)—both of which initiated adepts in ritual sex magick. [7]

It is also likely that Pike was instructed in sex magick ceremonies from the Luxor group, with his associate, the flamboyant occult con artist, Helena Blavatsky. Pike's system at its peak was thoroughly Satanic. Once again, on a specific point in which Taxil is supposed to have been inventing falsities, he was correct. What, then, of his public repudiation of his writings?

Some of Taxil's claims may have been exaggerated. For example, Taxil has the candidate for the Entered Apprentice (First) Degree pass the test of "Solomon's goat," in which the sap is told, "You will kneel down very low and you will have the honor of sucking one of the sacred teats of Solomon's goat." Taxil writes that the candidate "takes the desired position and when he opens his mouth, believing that they will present him a teat of a properly cleaned goat, they place against his lips the dirty back-side of a filthy buck." [8]

Other details seem equally bizarre, such as Pike's alleged account of a medium floating in the air, or an account of a wireless set which issued a flame as a signal: but this could reflect the type of crock which Pike retailed to his minions, as could a few of the other "fantastic" details. It is also possible that the exaggerations are from Taxil himself, working as a Masonic agent to inflate credulity only later to deflate it by casting doubt upon even authenticated testimony of Satanism in the masonic lodges. But let us not move too quickly: such details could also reflect disinformation deliberately fed to Taxil and others by lodge "brothers" determined to safeguard actual secrets, part of the Masonic maze of hoodwinking lower members.

---

[7] Not to be confused with the Rosicrucian Order based in San Jose, which is largely a lightweight mail-order version started by OTO man H. Spencer Lewis.

[8] Leo Taxil (Gabriel Jogand-Pages), *Masonry Exposed and Explained* (St. Louis, Missouri: Church Progress, 1891) p. 45.

There is a third scenario to consider. The alchemical "Must Be" or "Revelation of the Method" discovered by sleuth James Shelby Downard, whereby the Cryptocracy itself reveals some of its deepest secrets and then issues plausible denials or discredits its own source.

It would seem that some of Taxil's revelations do in fact reflect some highly unusual but actual masonic events. Masons revel in gadgetry, techno-Wizardry and Scientism (as distinct from God-ordained natural science), as part of their obsession with Alchemy and occult symbolism. Inventions, dazzling effects, and the pseudo-miraculous are part and parcel of the stagecraft of the Craft, which has among its spiritual ancestors the magicians of Pharaonic Egypt who tried to imitate Moses by conjuring snakes (and did so, at least in credible appearance).

To put spice into this sizzling stew, Crowley's secretary, Israel Regardie, testifies in his book *The Eye in the Triangle* to having seen a Palladium charter signed by Leo Taxil and Diana Vaughan. [9]

The charter to which Israel Regardie referred was the "United States Charter for The Palladian Order," and was not only purchased in Paris in 1894 by Mr. Clarke Walker, but bears more signatures than simply those of Leo Taxil and Diana Vaughan—including the signature of Dr. Bataille (a Taxil associate) and the very significant signature of 'Dr. W. Westcott." [10]

Dr. William Wynn Westcott was the founder of the Hermetic Order of the Golden Dawn, which suggests that the Palladium was not only real but tied to the Golden Dawn and the circles in which Crowley and Regardie lived and moved. Taxil's initial findings were seconded by other investigators, two of whom Waite claims also issued retractions. One of these, Dr. Bataille (a.k.a. Dr. Hacks), was reportedly visited by an interviewer who found him, according to Waite, "in a comfortable apartment above his

---

[9] Later, Regardie termed the charter fraudulent, without giving any basis for this conclusion, which runs counter to his earlier testimony.

[10] Louis T. Culling, *A Manual of Sex Magick*, quoted in Darcy Kuentz, *The Golden Dawn Source Book*, p. 134.

restaurant on the Boulevard Montmartre, where—by a pleasantry of its proprietor—the stained-glass windows exhibited heads of Lucifer." [11]

But Waite had already portrayed Dr. Bataille as an "absolute materialist and disbeliever in the supernatural" two pages earlier. Why then such a "pleasantry" as heads of Lucifer on stained glass windows? In addition, we might inquire why Waite goes out of his way to ridicule the notion of Luciferian Freemasonry when his own encyclopedia carries an illustration on page iv which is "said to typify the Morning Star or Lucifer, emerging from clouds"? Waite was a leader in the Golden Dawn, named after Lucifer. Waite wrote the *Book of Black Magic and Pacts*. Is it not Waite who is having his own "pleasantry," a Thelemic jest and hoax of his own devising?

In the end the mystery centers on Taxil's retraction, which was (as reported) a lengthy, detailed and exhaustive portrayal full of self-incrimination, which seemed to glory in the nature of the hoax which he supposedly pulled off just "for fun," allegedly making up the Palladium out of thin air.

Could Taxil have been a double or even a triple agent? If so, he certainly ran a brilliant, early-day black op campaign on behalf of the lodges, to discredit anti-masonic exposures with a "dirty tricks" campaign intended to nullify all attacks and exposés, while simultaneously leaking actual details of the most salacious and Satanic dimension of Palladium Freemasonry, as part of a diabolically clever psychological control-and-alibi mechanism embodied in the Downardian principle of Revelation of the Method.

Is something like the Palladium around today—other than the comparatively small-scale version allegedly revived by David DePaul? Has a sexually pathological and Satanic core of Scottish Rite Freemasonry continued to exist? Is this Palladium the OTO itself, which initiates its members into the occult rituals described by Pike as the "Rites of the Highest Masonry"?

Organizations such as the Palladium do not typically disappear, but they occasionally change appearance,

---

[11] Waite, *A New Encyclopedia of Freemasonry*, II, p. 257.

particularly when too much light is shone on them. To locate an equivalent of the Palladium within the modern Masonic spectrum, we only need to keep in mind a few defining characteristics described by Taxil and company:

The Palladium taught sex magick. It contained women as well as men. It worshipped Baphomet or the Goat of Mendes—popularly known as the devil. It was essentially a formal dogmatic religion. It was led by an inner circle of elites within high degrees of Scottish Rite Freemasonry. From written letters of leaders in both the Golden Dawn and the OTO, it is apparent that both Orders collaborated and intersected. [12]

If we examine the OTO, we will find that 1). it teaches sex magick, 2). it contains women as well as men, 3). it worships Baphomet, in the "Sixth Degree, the Illustrious Knights Templar of the Order of KADOSCH and of Dame Companions of the Order of the Holy Grail," where OTO Initiates hear the Grand Commander declare, "Behold our God, Baphomet, the unutterable one, the bearer of the Holy Grail"; 4). the OTO is officially registered as a religion with tax-exempt status; 5). the OTO was started by a high degree Freemason with charters in the various high degree rites 6). the OTO is, within esoteric Freemasonry, the only significant repository of occult ritual other than the Golden Dawn and its successor the *Argenteum Astrum* or AA (begun by Crowley) and 7). OTO leader Reuss collaborated closely with an alleged leader of the Palladium (Westcott).

Interestingly, Domenico Margiotta, one of the writers who claimed to have exposed the Palladium in the time of Taxil, wrote of a "Sovereign Universal Administrative Directory" originally headed by the revolutionary Freemason Guiseppe Mazzini, collaborating with Pike, which "Directory" was relocated to Berlin, Germany subsequent to Mazzini's death. Mazzini died in 1872.

If this is true, then Palladian Freemasonry shifted its center to Berlin, in Germany, where around 1880 Theodor Reuss ("Merlin Peregrinus") reactivated the Ludwig Lodge

---

[12] Photographs of this unique and important evidence are reproduced in the 1933 edition of the classic work, *Occult Theocracy* by "Lady Queenborough" (Edith Starr Miller).

of the Order of the Illuminati (the "OI," in Munich), and where Leopold Engel ("Theophrastus") founded the World League of the Illuminati circa 1893. These men joined forces and Reuss became the sole authority capable of founding and consecrating Masonic Lodges of the OI. Reuss also linked up with the Freemason Karl Kellner, establishing a German Grand Lodge of the highest ranking Orders of central European Freemasonry at that time, the "Rite of Memphis and Mizraim," which carried degrees upward to 97. Reuss established this lodge with two other occultists, Klein and Hartmann, in Berlin.

This Grand Lodge eventually issued a Masonic journal called *Oriflamme* in which the birth of the OTO was announced as the new Master Rite which included all Inner Sanctum "graduate" Freemasonry, including the degrees of the Illuminati. When Crowley traveled to see Reuss and receive his OTO appointment as leader of Great Britain, they met in Berlin.

Is it a coincidence that the Taxil-era literature describes the Palladium and directorship of Freemasonry as moving to Berlin approximately the same time the Illuminati is revived there and subsequently incorporated into the OTO? Is it a coincidence that in Berlin the OTO announces itself after its inception as the *Academia Masonica*—the Masonic Academy or Graduate School—as the new Master Rite of Freemasonry?

Taxil is historically interesting and even important, but not necessarily for lurid revelations of the perverse core of Freemasonry in its inner circles of squalor. For those choice spectacles we have ample testimony from Crowley and Kenneth Grant, both of whom brazenly announced much of the diabolical and depraved activities of the OTO. On the contrary, a revisionist reading of Taxil is important in order to rediscover the historical confluence of Freemasonry in its Palladian manifestation, and the modern organization of the OTO.

Is not the OTO the continuation and embodiment of the Palladium of Diana Vaughan, the "Graduate School" for salivating and serious Masons? We need look no further for the existence of the Palladium in our time than the Ordo Templi Orientis.

VI

Arcanum Arcanorum

"I am the Magician and the Exorcist."

Sex magick, which lies at the heart of top-level Freemasonry such as exists in the OTO is, of course, nothing new. As Sir James Frazier documents in *The Golden Bough*, such rites have been common around the world among primitives. In a clear but covert rabbinical lineage, the Zoharist Kabbalists held sex magick (or more correctly, "spermo-gnosticism") one of their most jealously guarded secrets, leading to a fusion of the male and female aspects of divinity, ultimately reducible to the Kabbalah's completed Androgynous being, "Adam Kadmon."

Rabbi Adin Steinsaltz quotes the Kabbalistic scripture *Tanya* of his Chabad-Lubavitcher sect of Hasidic Judaism, regarding the "vitality which is in the drops of semen...as is known to those who are familiar with the Esoteric Wisdom." Steinsaltz spends pages expounding these matters. [1] Kabbalah authority Daniel Matt of the Center for Judaic Studies at the Graduate Theological Union in Berkeley, California, explains the Zohar's teaching regarding sex in Zohar 1:49b-50a; 2:89a-b; 3:81a-b, and 168a. Matt quotes Rabbi Moses ben Jacob Cordovero, teacher of Isaac (a.k.a. Yitzhak) Luria: "Their desire, both his and hers, was to unite Shekhinah (the female deity). He focused on Tif'eret, and his wife on Malkhut ('spheres' of emanation from the Kabbalistic Adam Kadmon).

"His union was to join Shekhinah; she focused correspondingly on being Shekhinah and uniting with Her Husband, Tif'eret." Matt comments that this "corresponds to the Tantric ritual of *maithuna,* in which the human couple focuses on identification with their divine models..." [2]

---

[1] Adin Steinsaltz, *Opening the Tanya: Discovering the Moral & Mystical Teachings of a Classic Work of Kabbalah*, chapter seven.

[2] Daniel Matt, *Zohar: The Book of Enlightenment*, 236-237, Paulist Press edition.

Tantric Roots of Kabbalah

Tantric Yogis on the Indian subcontinent have practiced the secret techniques of sex magic for centuries. Michael A. Hoffman II, who researches occult symbolism and twilight language, and the pagan roots of rabbinic Judaism, comments on the preceding passage from Matt:

"Among the Bauls of Bengal and the Hinduized Ismai'ilis of western India, the gruesome sex magic of the left-hand path -- Tantra -- continues to this day. These defiling rituals, survivals of the *psychopathic sexualis* of the ancient Babylonians, Canaanites and Egyptians, have been considerably bowdlerized in contemporary New Age literature and advertised in resplendent terms as 'sacred sex that transcends mere coupling to ascend heights of tenderness and bliss.'

"While exploiting the prevailing ignorance of the authentic and unspeakable Tantric rituals, Daniel Matt concedes an important fact concerning the connection between Tantric and Kabbalistic rites, specifically in his reference to the Tantric act of *maithuna*.

"By doing so, Matt is confirming the pathological, pagan roots of Kabbalistic praxis. In Tantra, *maithuna* is one of the so-called 'Five M-Words' (the others are *matsya, mamsa, madya* and *mudra). Maithuna* literally denotes 'fornication' and when Matt confesses that Judaism's Kabbalah rite 'corresponds to the Tantric ritual of *maithuna,*' he is indicating that it is based upon the ancient Tantric practice of the ritual consumption of polluting substances, such as sexual and menstrual fluids and discharge during fornication, which is at the heart of the *maithuna* rite.

"The atrocious sexual sin of nations such as the Canaanites, which drew the wrath of Yahweh upon them, was the ceremonial perversion of human sexuality subject to the requirements of bestial temple magic. The formulas for these rites were transmitted through the ages by oral tradition, until committed to writing in the Kabbalah of Judaism and the Tantra of medieval south Asia." [3]

[3] Quoted by permission of the author from the manuscript of his forthcoming, expanded hardcover edition of *Judaism's Strange Gods* (first printed in 2000 in paperback), due for publication in the revised edition in 2006.

Kabbalah, like "Tantra" presents a false front of benevolence to the world, but is something else entirely in real life. This was hammered home in September of 2004 when the rock star Madonna arrived in the Israeli state to join 2,000 other New Age Kabbalists from 22 nations, for a *Rosh Hashanah* pilgrimage to the graves of the gentile-hating Kabbalists, Shimon ben Yohai and Yitzhak Luria. "These (the graves) are energy vortexes," explained Rabbi Shaul Youdkevitch, head of the Israeli Kabbalah Center. "It is known among Kabbalists that you can go there and recharge yourself with positive energy."

The "positive" vibes Madonna and her rabbi were attempting to promote for the Kabbalah contrasted rather poorly with another Kabbalistic event that occurred on the eve of Madonna's Israeli pilgrimage. Rabbi Yosef Dayan, from the West Bank settlement of Psagot, announced on Sept. 14, 2004, that if asked to hold a *Pulsa Denura,* a black magic Kabbalah ritual aimed at putting a death curse on Ariel Sharon, he would do so. Rabbi Dayan conducted a *Pulsa Denura* ceremony targeting former Israeli Prime Minister Yitzhak Rabin, prior to Rabin's assassination in 1995. The Kabbalistic ritual of *Pulsa Denura* is supposed to lead to the death of the ceremony's target. [4] So much for the "positive Kabbalah" hype.

The Gnostics were early rivals of the Christians who, together with the "sages" of Judaism's Talmud and Kabbalah, kept the Babylonian mysteries alive. The founder of Gnosticism is said to be Simon Magus, who seems like a forerunner of Pike's Palladium. In the words of St. Irenaeus of Lyons, "Now Simon, the Samaritan, from whom all heresies got their start, proposed the following sort of heretical doctrine. Having himself redeemed a certain Helen from being a prostitute in Tyre, a city of Phoenicia, he took her with him on his rounds...(his followers) do whatever they will, since they are free...The mystic priests of these people live licentious lives and practice magic, each one in whatever way he can." [5]

This blend of occultism and sex never quite died even

---

[4] Haaretz News Service, Sept. 14, 2004.
http://www.haaretz.com/hasen/spages/477956.html
[5]

Irenaeus, *Against the Heresies,* Book I, Chapter XXIII.

in the era of Christendom, surviving underground in various ways, notably with the help of the most zealous rabbis. It surfaced again in what was originally a Christian Order, the Knights Templars of the Twelfth Century. Surprisingly, these warrior-monks were eventually condemned by the Church for worshipping Baphomet and practicing sodomy—later said by occultists to be "advanced" sex magick.

The mainstream Masonically-spun version of the affair states that all of this is nonsense; that the Church made a power grab, tortured the Templar leaders into a bogus confession, and burned their Grand Master Jacques De Molay in an act of supreme cruelty. [6]

But not all confessions were extracted by torture, and many of the Knights who admitted to these actions were spared. These facts are admitted by Michael Howard, whose comparatively candid pen reflects some objective spade work. In spite of some errors, Howard managed to avoid the trendy occultist tendency to blame the Church for every evil under the sun, if not also for any defects in the moon and stars as well. The fact of the matter is that the Templar tradition is well known in occult circles as the initiated tradition of sex magick, pure and simple. De Molay was no innocent martyr (significantly, the Masonic club for young boys is the Order of De Molay—named after the above demonic pedophile).

Arcanum Arcanorum

As we saw in the last chapter, Taxil's Palladium described one more outcropping of this initiated current, a current which tended to hide in secret societies from the vigilant and at times hostile gaze of the Church. Hence, the creation of Freemasonry, one more haven, hidden from view, with an elaborate system of initiation which functioned as a screen to keep most of the members in the

---

[6] This masonic propaganda about DeMolay has even been embraced by Catholic writers such as Sandra Miesel, writing in *The Da Vinci Hoax: Exposing the Errors in The Da Vinci Code* (in which she briefly mentions the OTO while misspelling its name in Latin). Miesel parrots the Masonic account of DeMolay and treats conspiracies with the usual scorn. Her book was issued by Ignatius Press, a neo-con Catholic publishing house.

dark, and to advance only those deemed sufficiently processed to be made ready for an encounter with Templarism. Various occult lodges existed for the practice of this higher Freemasonry, that is, the esoteric and occult core, or Magick.

Freemasons like to boast that they worship the Christian God under the title of "the Great Architect." They suppress an important distinction, however. In Biblical theology God always creates *ex nihilo*—from nothing—and is therefore not an "architect" who merely arranges pre-existing material. Whereas the serpent, Satan, is a created being who must work with that which is given. Therefore, the "Great Architect" which the Masons honor cannot be the God of the Bible.

The supreme secret, the *Arcanum Arcanorum*, was always sex magick and semen-worship. But there is more. Initiation includes repeated invocation, or "calling in" various spirits, over and over, until one is identified with them, in other words, possessed by them. The ultimate gnosis contained within the Third Degree Ritual of the Blue Lodge (but never understood by the so-called "Master Mason") was gradually taught by these spirits: that it is man himself who is God; man who is the "Great Architect of the Universe." As it is written in *Liber Oz, the Book of the Goat* of the OTO, "There is no god but man."

Blue Lodge Masonry hints at this secret when it teaches that the initiate has "resurrected" himself in the Third Degree ritual, and thus he is made to proclaim (often without realizing it) his own divinity as the risen divine Master, a type of Antichrist. This Master Mason Degree is a kind of occult Mass, in which one must "transubstantiate" one's own consciousness, accepting that there is no God, and simultaneously, therefore, each is his own god. In this way the Mason can worship anything as divine, including the devil, because everything is equal to the total, which is also equal to Nothing, the *Ain Sof* of the Kabbalah, the "light of limitless nothingness." It is this mystical hubris, together with tranquil acceptance of cosmic despair, which, according to masonic doctrine, is the "light" brought about by the Great Architect Lucifer, with whose viewpoint the Freemasonic initiate will eventually consciously identify.

Pike taught in the 32nd Degree that occult science is found in the rites of the Highest Masonry, where "it is humanity that creates God; and men think that God has made them in His image, because they make Him in theirs." He further stated that the "Secret of the Occult Sciences" was given to the human race by the Devil, when in the Garden of Eden he said, Ye shall be like the *Elohim* (as gods), knowing good and evil: "...it was this same remembrance, preserved, or perhaps profaned in the celebrated Order of the Templars, that became for all the secret associations, of the Rose-Croix, of the Illuminati, and of the Hermetic Freemasons, the reason of their strange rites, of their signs more or less conventional, and, above all, of their mutual devotedness and of their power."

The Templar tradition, then, was the surviving current of occultism and sex magick, used to "initiate" people into the denial of God, the affirmation of themselves as absolute rulers of their own lives, and the veneration of Baphomet or Satan.

Here is one more twist in the OTO-Masonic maze of deception. Remember that the Masonic Light is meant to blind, as Pike remarked. The illusion of self-rulership and divinity is used as an intoxicating drug to inoculate followers and dupes both in the lodges and outside the lodge (the so-called "Masons without an Apron"), into believing themselves above possible enslavement, as too omnipotent and omniscient to be yoked and deceived. We have seen how the OTO points to a totalitarian regime; similarly, Pike's Templar Degree relates how "the World will soon come to us for its Sovereigns and Pontiffs. We shall constitute the equilibrium of the Universe, and be rulers over the Masters of the World." [7]

---

[7] Albert Pike, *Morals and Dogma*, p. 817.

VII

The Judaic Connection

"For the good of Masonry, generally, but the Jewish nation in particular." Royal Arch Degree of Freemasonry

The wealthy Austrian industrialist Karl Kellner decided around 1895 to pass on his own initiation into Tantric yoga to an inner circle of followers. Kellner's accomplice Theodor Reuss, a fanatical Anglo-German Freemason, bought Masonic charters in every High Degree he could lay his hands on. By 1902 Reuss had imported Scottish Rite and Memphis and Mizraim Freemasonry to Germany. Kellner occupied himself with "yoga" and Memphis and Mizraim Masonry. Reuss and Kellner conceived of a new Outer Order through which they could select Masons for training in Kellner's trumpeted concoction of Tantra. At the same time Reuss had revived the old Order of the Illuminati, said to have started in Bavaria by "Adam Weishaupt" in 1776 and later grafted onto Grand Orient Freemasonry. Reuss also worked with the Societas Rosicruciana in Anglia (from which came the Hermetic Order of the Golden Dawn), and Martinism (French Illuminist Masonry). Reuss was also linked in its early years to Blavatsky's Theosophical Society through Franz Hartmann.

But it would be a mistake to see the OTO as an essentially German occult phenomenon grafted onto a bloody Tantric sex magick. The pivotal source for Reuss was the sex-magickal Hermetic Brotherhood of Light (also known as Luxor), a secret society which included Madame Blavatsky and "Papus," the advisor to Czar Nicholas of Russia. As Jocelyn Godwin and his co-researchers observe, the teachings of the Hermetic Brotherhood of Light (H. B. of L.), "fed the streams of sexual practice flowing in the Ordo Templi Orientis of Theodor Reuss and eventually into the works of Aleister Crowley. Once the secret was out, linking occultism with sex, it was impossible to ignore, and in consequence, practically every occult order after the

1880s has some debt to the H. B. of L." [1]

But whose secret was it? "Max Theon" ("Supreme God") was Grand Master of the Egyptian Hermetic Brotherhood of Light in the 1870s. Theon lived in a vast villa named Zarif near Tlemcen in Algeria. A frequent visitor to England and France, Theon's true name was Louis Maximilian Bimstein. Bimstein was the son of Rabbi Judes Lion Bimstein of Warsaw, Poland. Godwin writes, "One concludes that Theon must have spent much of his existence under false names or false identity papers, and that he did not hesitate to give wrong information to the authorities." Theon/Bimstein was initiated at age eighteen in Hasidic Judaism before he left Poland. He also gained initiation into Kabbalah.

The wealthy Jacob Frank, originally Jacob Leibowicz, stressed the Zohar ("Book of Radiance" or "Splendor"), the most important text of the Kabbalah in Judaism. While the Talmud codified the bureaucratic side of Judaism, the Kabbalah conveyed the mysticism of black magic. The Zohar taught of a sexual split within God, the integration of which required intercourse and Judaic conquest. Frank emphasized the sexual teaching, although he certainly did not originate it, as maintained by current rabbinical disinformation. [2]

Nightside of Eden

A few Orthodox rabbis have made a pretext of opposing the Kabbalah, and Kabbalah opposition has been ascribed to Rabbi Moses Maimonides, but according to Michael A. Hoffman II, this is a hoax intended for gentile consumption: "The alleged opposition or incompatibility

---

[1] Jocelyn Godwin, Christian Chanel, John P. Deveney, *The Hermetic Brotherhood of Luxor,* p. 67.

[2] Because Frank was a heretic, the Kabbalah initiation he provided others has been labeled by Orthodox Judaism as spurious. Whatever Frank's personal beliefs, however, the Kabbalistic teaching he imparted was consonant with mainstream Orthodox instruction. For more on Frank cf. T Allen Greenfield, "The Frankist Ecstatics of the Eighteenth Century," in *Agape: The Official Organ of the U.S. Grand Lodge of Ordo Templi Orientis,* Vol. 1, Issue 2, February 1998

between Kabbalistic Judaism and, for example, the halachic Judaism of Maimonides is a fallacy. Maimonides was revered by many of the seminal Kabbalists of all time, including Rabbi Haim David Azulai, Rabbi Gershon Henoch of Radzin, Rabbi Yitzhak (the Komarno Rebbe), and the preeminent Kabbalist, Rav Abraham Abulafia (a formative influence on Moses Cordevero and Haim Vital). Abulafia esteemed Maimonides' famous book, *The Guide of the Perplexed* as a Kabbalistic text."

The Kabbalah is considered advanced Judaism for the few, as Rabbi Adin Steinsaltz writes in *The Essential Talmud*, p. 212: "...there was a whole world of mysticism and mystery that was concealed from the general public and transmitted only to a chosen few...These esoteric subjects were therefore taught by the rabbi to only one chosen disciple and, in some cases, the teacher confined himself to the outlines of the subject without going into detail...The stringent restrictions on esoteric interpretation were relaxed gradually during the Middle Ages...By the beginning of the modern era, the Kabbalah (literally tradition, transmittal) was an important and even central element in Jewish thought. Much of what we can surmise of the esoteric world of the talmudic sages is based on this literature and the light it casts on the hints contained in the Talmud."

The occult is extolled in the Kabbalah as a necessary "descent" to complete one's transformation. According to the rabbinic lies told about the patriarch Abraham, he made his "descent" (according to Zohar 1:81b) and "had to know all those levels that are connected below," which Daniel Matt calls the "dark underside of wisdom" and which Matt candidly links not to the wisdom of the God of Israel, but to the gnosis of the magicians of pagan Egypt:

"This wisdom of Egypt includes magic and alchemy. Abraham's descent symbolizes his exploration of *Sitra Abra*, 'the Other Side,' the Abyss. This dangerous psychic journey is the crucible of Abraham's spiritual transformation."[3]

This "psychic journey" is called by Kenneth Grant the "Nightside of Eden," the negative side of the Lurianic

---

[3] Matt, op. cit. p. 220.

"Tree of Life" and it requires of the initiate, the full embrace of the demonic. The essential teachings of the Kabbalah were summarized by the late Professor Israel Shahak, of Hebrew University, Jerusalem:

"From the First Cause, first a male god called 'Wisdom' or "Father" and then a female goddess called "Knowledge" or 'Mother' were emanated or born. From the marriage of these two, a pair of younger gods were born: Son, also called by many other names such as 'Small Face' or 'The Holy Blessed One,' and Daughter, also called 'Lady' (or 'Matronit,' a word derived from Latin), 'Shekhinah,' 'Queen,' and so on.

"These two younger gods should be united, but their union is prevented by the machinations of Satan, who in this system is a very important and independent personage...The creation of the Jewish people was undertaken in order to mend the break caused by Adam and Eve, and under Mount Sinai this was for a moment achieved: the male god Son, incarnated in Moses, was united with the goddess Shekhinah...The Jewish conquest of Palestine from the Canaanites and the building of the first and second Temple are particularly propitious for their union....

"The duty of pious Jews is to restore through their prayers and religious acts the perfect divine unity, in the form of sexual union, between the male and female deities. Thus before most ritual acts, which every devout Jew has to perform many times each day, the following cabbalistic formula is recited: 'For the sake of the (sexual) congress of the Holy Blessed One and his Shekhinah...' The Jewish morning prayers are also arranged so as to promote this sexual union, if only temporarily. Successive parts of the prayer mystically correspond to successive stages of the union: at one point the goddess approaches with her hand-maidens, at another the god puts his arm around her neck and fondles her breast, and finally the sexual act is supposed to take place...." [4]

From the preceding passage, one can see that the Frankist sexual teaching is not spurious "red Kabbalah", but rather a legitimate part of the system of occult

---

[4] Israel Shahak, *Jewish History, Jewish Religion.*

integration which the Zohar teaches will lead to both a completed deity and a completed Judaic male, which are ultimately one and the same.

Louis Bimstein ("Max Theon"), took this secret and disseminated it, omitting certain other facets of the Kabbalah, such as the teaching that Gentiles are the "limbs of Satan."

In Rabbi Adin Steinsaltz's study of the *Tanya* of Shneur Zalman, the founder of the Chabad-Lubavtich branch of Hasidic Judaism, we read that "...the second soul of the Jew is a part of God above, literally," while "The souls of the nations of the world, however, derive from the other impure *kelipot* (demonic 'shells'), which contain no good whatever, as it is written in Etz Chayyim, Portal 49, ch. 3..." [5]

The old Hermetic Brotherhood of Light worked as a means of "occulturating" the masses -- giving them a few tidbits of the Kabbalah while withholding the real secrets, similar to the "Kabbalah Centre" of Rabbi Yehuda Berg, one of the mentors of Madonna and Britney Spears. By this means, occultists and New Agers could believe they had reached the advanced secrets of the Kabbalah, while in reality Bimstein and others withheld key teachings, including the doctrine of the non-humanity of the gentiles.

From this double-minded double-cross rose the supposedly final Masonic revelations which were systematized by Reuss. Kellner fell terminally ill in 1904 and Reuss, excited by the Kabbalistic secrets, began recruiting members of Scottish Rite and Memphis-Mizraim Freemasonry (also sexual in its advanced degrees), for a new, emerging Order. Kellner died the following year. By 1906 the Order had crystallized into the Ordo Templi Orientis. Soon Reuss' Masonic publication the *Oriflamme* announced the OTO. Eventually Reuss claimed that all of the secret knowledge of High Degree Freemasonry had been distilled by the OTO into a system of eleven degrees. The first three degrees were essentially similar to any Blue Lodge. The fourth through the sixth degrees captured the most important and powerful points of initiation in nearly all High Degree systems: the Royal

[5] *Opening the Tanya: Discovering the Moral & Mystical Teachings of a Classic Work of Kabbalah*, 68-70.

Arch, Rose-Croix, and Kadosch rituals. The seventh degree furnished theory for the eighth and ninth degrees, which consist of sex-magick (the eighth involves "magickal masturbation" and the ninth, coitus—the "Sanctuary of the Gnosis"). The tenth degree conferred administration over a country ("Supreme and Holy King"), while the eleventh contained a homosexual version of the ninth.

Judaism: Master Key to the Occult

In spite of his trappings mentioning "Gnostic Christianity," Reuss' instructions were based on the Kabbalah of the rabbis, which in fact preceded and inspired the early Gnostic heresies. The antiquity of the Kabbalah has been confirmed by Prof. Moshe Idel, of Hebrew University (cf. *Kabbalah: New Perspectives*). The *Jewish Encyclopedia* states concerning gnosticism: "Jewish gnosticism unquestionably antedates Christianity...Magic, also...was a not unimportant part of the doctrines and manifestations of gnosticism, (which) largely occupied Jewish thinkers...It is a noteworthy fact that heads of Gnostic schools and founders of Gnostic systems are designated as Jews by the Church Fathers. Some derive all heresies, including those of gnosticism, from Judaism."

Rabbi Bimstein's son was the hidden source of the "Germanic" OTO forerunner which was supposedly derived from Sufi initiations. The real roots are clear as reflected in this typical line from Reuss' instructions: "If the youth is mature, then he will complete the first coitus under the direction and instruction of the 'Matrona' (High Priestess) in a ritual manner and in the form of a 'Sacramental act.' Just the same will the virgin be introduced...." This is the language of the Zohar. It became the basis for Aleister Crowley's enthusiastic "Nightside of Eden" practice of corrupting men, women and boys with his "sacramental act."

Reuss advocated forced labor and genetic selection so that only "perfect parents" would produce children. Reuss dreamed of the OTO becoming the official state religion. These early facts about the OTO run counter to the libertarian mythology retailed to both inquiring outsiders and even most members today.

B'nai B'rith, Shin Bet and the OTO

The OTO is the successor to Freemasonry but it remains subordinate to Judaism, as all Masons are also subordinate, in keeping with the words of the Royal Arch Degree: "For the good of Masonry, generally, but the Jewish nation in particular." [6]

The system from its conception was ideologically related to totalitarian control systems reflecting Kabbalistic schemes for the *tikkun* or reintegration of Adam Kadmon, the divine male, through the capture of Palestine and the establishment of world rule according to the principles of the Zohar.

Friedrich Nietzsche observed, "The Jews are the most remarkable people in the history of the world, for when they were confronted with the question, to be or not to be, they chose, with perfectly unearthly deliberation, to be at any price: this price involved a radical falsification of all nature, of all naturalness, of all reality, of the whole inner world, as well as of the outer...one by one they distorted religion, civilization, morality, history and psychology until each became a contradiction of its natural significance."

This tendency Christ sought to overturn, but it survived as a mentality, a religion of the Double Mind, gradually named Judaism. It gathered European converts from the 8th century kingdom of Khazaria, forming the basis of the impostor "Jews" spoken of in Revelation 2:9, the Khazars who say they are Jews and are not. This racial masquerade complements a Judaic mentality of duplicity and falsification which was then carried into Christendom, sewing the seeds which would gradually produce the contradictions which are at the heart of the OTO and modern culture. [7]

A key operative at work in the establishment of the OTO was the "Jewish refugee" and B'nai B'rith activist, Dr. Felix Lazerus Pinkus (1881-1947), a major player in

---

[6] *Duncan's Masonic Ritual and Monitor*, p. 249.

[7] For more on the Khazars cf. Paul Wexler, *The Ashkenazic Jews: A Slavo-Turkic People in Search of a Jewish Identity*, (Columbus, Ohio: Slavica Press, 1993) and Kevin Alan Brook, *The Jews of Khazaria* (Jason Aronson, 1999).

the Zionist movement as president of the Zurich Union of Zionists. In 1918 he published, *On the Founding of a Jewish State,* subsequently becoming an economic expert for the Soviet Union's Trade Delegation in Switzerland. Pinkus was also active in the B'nai B'rith Lodge.

The exclusively Judaic B'nai B'rith was founded in 1843 by Jewish members of the Masons and other secret societies, such as Isaac Roenbourg, William Renau, and Reuben Rodacher. As B'nai B'rith leader Edward Grusd writes, "There is a legend, which is occasionally mentioned to this day, that B'nai B'rith was founded because in 1843 Jews were barred from membership in the Masonic orders and the Odd Fellows. Obviously, that was not the case, since several of the Order's founders were themselves members of those organizations. We have fragments of memoirs written by Rosenbourg, and Renau, as well as by others who joined B'nai B'rith soon after it was founded, which leave no doubt about this." [8]

Pinkus was the "spiritual father" of Hermann Joseph Metzger ("Frater Paragranus,"1919-1990), himself a later head of the OTO in Switzerland. Pinkus initiated Metzger in the degrees of the OTO up to IX, the peak of ordinary initiation. Metzger was also initiated into the secrets of master hypnotist and "magnetist" Anton Mesmer by Pinkus. Metzger became known as a conjurer under the alias Peter Mano, (a pun on the renowned stage hypnotist Hermano). Metzger went on to lead the Swiss branch of the OTO and the Order of the Illuminati or Ordo Illuminatorum (OI), fulfilling Reuss' dream of Illuminati revival to some extent. With Metzger's prominence, what status must we assign to Pinkus, his "spiritual father?" Evidently a great deal, although most histories of the OTO today ignore him completely, preferring to speak of alleged Sufi influences which have never been documented. [9]

---

[8] Grusd, *B'nai B'rith: The Story of a Covenant,* pp. 12-14.

[9] Sufism represents the mystical side of Islam, though it is considered heretical by most Islamic fundamentalists. Sufism is known in western culture mainly through the poetry of Rumi and the ecstatic dance of the Whirling Dervishes. As with the Kabbalistic rabbis, the graves of Sufi masters are regarded as places of power. Cf. Carl W. Ernst, *Sufism* (Boston: Shambhala, 1997), pp. 72-74.

Another fascinating and secretive figure on the OTO landscape is Oscar R. Schlag (1907-1991), an associate of the pioneering psychologist, Dr. Carl Gustav Jung. While not a member himself, Schlag nonetheless moved within several upper echelon OTO circles, visiting Jane Wolfe in 1955 at the California Lodge led by Jet Propulsion Laboratory rocket scientist Jack Parsons. Schlag was an intimate associate of top OTO men such as Karl Germer, and belonged to the "Abramelin group" which also contained Pinkus. Marcelos Motta, leader of the OTO in Brazil, learned through his own contacts in Brazilian intelligence that Schlag was in the employ of the psychological warfare section of the Israeli Shin Bet intelligence service, as well as the CIA. Motta became alarmed when the OTO allegedly staged a "courtroom coup" and ousted Motta from "legal standing" in the OTO in the eyes of the United States. Motta was convinced the CIA was controlling the OTO behind the scenes through Schlag.

Friedrich Levke (1904-1956) was yet another personification of the Judaic-OTO intersection. An initiate of the IX degree and friend of Aleister Crowley, Levke merged Thelema with Hasidic Judaism and became a friend of Hasidic propagandist Martin Buber, who conveniently omitted from his numerous books in praise of Hasidic sages, any mention of the central belief of Hasidic Judaism (as noted in reference to Zalman's *Tanya*), that the vast majority of Gentiles are purely evil, sub-human creatures. Subsidized by the California Agape Lodge of the OTO, Levke became known as Rebbe (Rabbi) Sair.

Master Rite of the Cryptocracy

As early in its history as 1917, the year of the Bolshevik Revolution in Russia, the OTO was announcing itself as the new Master Rite of occult and Masonic initiation. In the *Manifesto*, the OTO proclaimed itself to be, "...a body of initiates in whose hands are concentrated the wisdom and the knowledge of the following bodies:

1. The Gnostic Catholic Church.
2. The Order of the Knights of the Holy Ghost.
3. The Order of the Illuminati.
4. The Order of the Temple (Knights Templar).

5. The Order of the Knights of St. John.
6. The Order of the Knights of Malta. [10]
7. The Order of the Knights of the Holy Sepulchre.
8. The Hidden Church of the Holy Gail.
9. The Hermetic Brotherhood of Light.
10. The Holy Order of Rose Croix of Heredom.
11. The Order of the Holy Royal Arch of Enoch.
12. The Antient and Primitive Rite of Masonry (33 degrees).
13. The Rite of Memphis (97 degrees).
14. The Rite of Mizraim (90 degrees).
15. The Ancient and Accepted Scottish Rite of Masonry (33 degrees).
16. The Swedenborgian Rite of Masonry.
17. The Order of the Martinists.
18. The Order of the Sat Bhai.

"The dispersion of the original secret wisdom having led to confusion, it was determined by the Chiefs of all these Orders to recombine and centralize their activities...its chiefs are initiates of the highest rank, and recognized as such by all capable of such recognition in every country in the world...The Order is international, and has existing branches in every civilized country of the world...The OTO..(is) an *Academia Masonica*..."

Whether or not every claim in the preceding *Manifesto* was literally true, the announcement was clear for those with eyes to see: a thoroughly Judaic OTO had stepped forth as the new Master Rite of the Cryptocracy.

To a youthful Aleister Crowley, this claim became irresistible. And it is irresistible to many today, who seek arcana in dark rooms amid sexual indulgence and statues of Baphomet, unaware of any governing shadows emanating from the CIA, Shin Bet, or B'nai B'rith.

Not only did the OTO have important roots and ties to Zionist and governmental Overlords, the Golden Dawn left similar hoofprints. As Golden Dawn scholar Gareth J. Medway writes, "The Golden Dawn initiatory system is rather like a Jewish adaptation of the Scottish Rite (which is sometimes called 'Rose Croix Masonry', because the 18th

---

[10] Historically, the Knights of Malta were rivals of the Templars. There is an ongoing debate concerning whether the Malta group is part of the masonic network.

degree, the most important is Rosicrucian.) In the Zelator Grade the Neophyte is taken to the 'Holy Place', which contains representations of a seven-pointed star representing the seven-branched candlestick, circles equivalent to the Tribes of Israel, and the Altar of Incense. All this is certainly based in the 23rd degree of the Scottish Rite, called 'Chief of the Tabernacle', which is set in the Tabernacle of Moses in the desert as described in the Book of Exodus." [11]

Medway entertains circumstantial evidence that the Golden Dawn was linked to the Judaic Masonic Lodge in Frankfurt, Germany, known as *L'Aurore naissant* or *Loge zur aufgehenden Morgenroete*, founded in 1808. This lodge negotiated with Carl von Hessen, Landgrave of Schleswig, for patronage. In return, he insisted that they institute the higher Scottish Rite degrees, but some tension occurred over the gnostic, pseudo-Christian content of some of these Scottish Rite degrees; blasphemous as these references and aspects would be to orthodox Christians, they were still too much for the Judaics, who considered instituting instead a 'parallel structure' with more overtly Judaic references. Medway sees in the Golden Dawn just such a Christ-shorn, Judiasm-oriented parallel structure, and hence considers initial Golden Dawn ties to the Jewish Lodge in Frankfurt to be likely.

In any case, the Judaic Masonic Lodge was approved by the Grand Lodge of England, and so received the tolerant British Imprimatur of the power behind church and state in that land.

The Rosicrucian/Masonic encyclopedist Kenneth H. Mackenzie wrote in his 1877 *Royal Masonic Cyclopaedia,* of a secret Kabbalah college in London under the direction of one Johann Friedrich Falk, whom Mackenzie claimed was the son of the "Baalshem of London," Dr. Hayim Samuel Jacob Falk, (a.k.a. Caïn Chenul Falk), a Kabbalist known for his necromantic pursuit of the spirits of the dead. [12]

---

[11] Quoted by Darcy Kuentz, *The Golden Dawn Sourcebook,* p. 166.

[12] *Baalshem*: a title conferred upon rabbis who have mastered the "72 Kabbalistic Names of God" by which they attempt to work magic.

Dr. Falk not only carried weight with the Judaic establishment in London, he was also was internationally influential with Judaic and Gentile Freemasons, and was described by the Abbé Fournier as "the chief of all the Jews." His cult-following extended to the nobility, including Prince Czartoryski of Poland and the Duke of Orleans, who consulted Falk on his chances of becoming King of France. Falk's prestige was an indication of the status of Judaic Kabbalists among the London Freemasons who, while claiming to be a "Christians only" organization, secretly welcomed Judaics as members, including Rabbi Baruch ben Jacob of Shklov, a leading figure in the liberal "Jewish Enlightenment" (Haskalah).

In such an overtly Judaic milieu, it is natural that Dr. Falk's above-mentioned son, Johann Falk, would possess the prestige to mentor, through his Kabbalistic college, the heads of the Golden Dawn. Indeed this college was explicitly claimed as the source of the Hermetic Order of the Golden Dawn by Golden Dawn founder William W. Westcott, who wrote of it as "the order of mystics which gave Eliphas Lévi...his occult knowledge." [13]

Although Crowley outgrew the Golden Dawn, he used its material to form his own Kabbalistic-Rosicrucian school, the Order of the Silver Star (Argenteum Astrum or AA). Crowley's modifications were to change the initiation from a group basis to individual training, and to give far greater prominence to Tantric "disciplines" as Crowley had experienced them in India. The AA still exists today as the second Order of the Cult of the Beast, and purports to take its adherents to "deeper" levels of initiation, that is, it creates megalomaniacs who carry on the inner Masonic traditions of the Kabbalah as derived from Judaism and its petrie dish of occultism which it has successfully preserved for millennia.

The late Rabbi Aryeh Kaplan explains the occult practices of the Kabbalah in the introduction to his translation of the oldest Kabbalah scripture, the Sefer

---

[13] Cf. Ron Heisler, "Precursors of the Golden Dawn" in Darcy Kuentz, The Golden Dawn Sourcebook, pp. 115-119. Heisler exhibits some skepticism toward the claims regarding Johann Falk and the Kabbalistic college, but not of the general fact of important Judaic influence on the Golden Dawn."

Yetzirah ("Book of Creation"): "The third category of Kabbalah --the magical---consists of various signs, incantations and divine names, through which one can influence or alter natural events...the most important texts have never been printed, although some fragments have been published. One of the best examples of these is the book Raziel." [14]

The book referred to by Kaplan is the *Sefer Rezial (Razial) Hemelach,* the Book of the Angel Rezial, which is a secret rabbinic grimoire, a prototype of the "Enochian Calls" of John Dee. The *Sefer Rezial* contains the *Sefer Hamezeloth,* the Book of the Signs of the Zodiac, as well as prescriptions for making amulets and talismans, still popular in the Israeli state due to the official status of Orthodox Judaism as the state religion.

A typical passage of this heavily suppressed rabbinical text is the following: "When pigs or goats have sexual intercourse, the males with the females are able to produce. Cease the sexual intercourse to make strong. Also, when desired to make use of, or when dirty by places of the sea, or mud and clay, desire to be very dirty. Also, desire pleasures and seek pleasure from below the earth, until the ends of the opening edges." [15]

The official cover story emanating from the Grand Lodge of England is that the OTO and the AA are not "regular" Masonry. The Blue Lodge Masons who have imbibed such drivel should read, besides the works of their own leaders, John J. Robinson's book, *Born in Blood* (chapter seven) and wake up to the fact that the Kabbalistic tradition as practiced by the Templars and carried down to the lodges, is at the heart of the Masonic system and always has been. It logically follows that one's depth of initiation and understanding of arcana in Freemasonry is measured by immersion in the Kabbalah.

To initiates, proof that the Beast Cult, as spread by the OTO, became the elite Master Rite, is the fact that no "occult war" is known to have occurred after the OTO claimed such a privilege. Such wars typically would have broken out, replete with occult Masons siccing devils on

---

[14] Aryeh Kaplan, *Sefer Yetzirah: The Book of Creation*, p. x.

[15] *Sefer Rezial Hemelach*, Book "Berashith," part two.

each other through Kabbalistic conjurations. But nothing like that has transpired. Intertwined with Judaism and US and Israeli intelligence, the OTO burrowed into its role and grew throughout the West, essentially unchallenged. While other powerful, cognate occult groups, such as Skull and Bones, certainly exert enormous power, none has the indisputable position in the world today which belongs to the OTO as the Judaically-anointed leader of the modern Beast Cult of the Kabbalah, and thereby of blood, control, deception, and death.

VIII

Catholicism in the Crosshairs

"With my Hawk's head I peck at the eyes of Jesus as he hangs upon the cross."

One of Aleister Crowley's early projects was the creation of a Gnostic Mass for the OTO. He called it the original "pre-Christian Christianity," a mocking reference to the fact that his rite was created with a special intention. Not content with a mere reversal of the Mass, like the typical Black Mass of traditional Satanism, Crowley wished to replace Christianity, not only rebel against it. This desire for replacement is enshrined in this rite, which reflects a Zoharic sexual orientation most likely of Frankist transmission as handed down from Louis Bimstein.

But why would Crowley study the Roman Catholic Mass, as he did in creating his rite? Why the obsession with Catholicism? The Cult of the Beast has its place within a current of historical momentum which originated long before Crowley was fascinated with a woman's blood. The OTO surfed upon a board fashioned by older hands. It is at the service of Elders with ancient traditions and ancestral hatreds.

To properly interpret the phenomenon of the Gnostic Mass, we must look at the elder secret societies which have sheltered deviltry in various forms. The OTO's mention of blood upon an altar is no accident: there are those who have longed for many centuries for certain altars to be drenched with consecrated blood, and occasionally achieved it.

The Legend of the Alta Vendita

In 1818, an Italian document supposedly fell into the wrong hands and was published: the "Permanent Instructions" for the heads of the highest grades of Freemasonry. The original Italian text was said to have been given in 1824 to "Nubio," one of the Supreme *Vendita* of the "Alta Vendita" Lodge of the Carbonari Freemasons, when he was sent to Rome to put the plans into effect. After the document was somehow supposedly "lost," Freemasons--as the story goes--allegedly offered fantastic sums for its recovery but were too late, a copy had reached the Pope. [1]

Eighteen days prior to his death on May 13, 1846, Pope Gregory XVI is said to have placed this document in the hands of Maurice Cretineau-Joly, who published them in his 1858 work, *L'Eglise Romaine en face de la Revolution* ("The Roman Church Facing the Revolution"), allegedly by order of Pope Pius IX. The originals are said to be archived in the Vatican, but this is purely speculation.

Monsignor George F. Dillon included extended passages from this "Alta Vendita" document in his lectures at Edinburgh in October, 1884. Apparently Pope Leo XIII was so pleased with these lectures that he paid from his own pocket to have them published and circulated, and they duly appeared in 1885 under the title, *The War of Antichrist With The Church and Christian Civilization.*

But are they genuine? Masons (naturally) say no; some Catholics say yes. Lacking the original autographs, the case rests mainly on anecdote and conjecture.

Given the broad canvas of Masonic statements, the Alta Vendita documents, while more than usually explicit, certainly blend into the large painting of their ambitions done by lodges over the years. These documents were trumpeted by Pope Leo XIII for obvious reasons, but it should be noted that by that time the pope had other material in his hands from which to quote—including Albert Pike's *Morals and Dogma* which was issued in 1871. It is safe to assume that Leo XIII had access to such things. The Alta Vendita documents are an elaboration of themes from other bona fide occult sources. Furthermore, other plans of secret societies which have surfaced—from Weishaupt's Illuminati to Crowley's Liber CCC—are of a similar vein.

A perusal of these documents should give pause to occultists—particularly Thelemites who see themselves as the champions of liberty and tolerance, the guardians of freedom to "Do What Thou Wilt." Yes, Thelemites and Freemasons of every stripe frequently complain that the Catholic Church has been stubborn, jealous, and intolerant in denouncing Freemasonry. While the Catholic

---

[1] How this top secret document came to be lost is never documented in the standard accounts of this legend. Why did Freemasons believe that offering a reward might recover it? No one knows. How the document fell into the hands of the pope is also unknown.

Church has at times lamentably been in the hands of churchmen who have betrayed higher interests and trampled upon the innocent, nevertheless the old antagonism of the Church toward Freemasonry is quite understandable if one reads a few translated quotations from the Alta Vendita: "Our final aim is that of Voltaire and of the French Revolution—the complete annihilation of Catholicism, and ultimately of Christianity. Were Christianity to survive, even upon the ruins of Rome, it would, a little later on, revive and live. The Pope, whoever he may be, will never enter into a secret society. It then becomes the duty of the Secret Society to make the first advance to the Church and to the Pope, with the object of conquering both. The work for which we gird ourselves up, is not the work of a day, nor of a month, nor of a year.

"It may last for many years, perhaps for a century; in our ranks the soldier dies, but the war is continued. We do not at present intend to gain the Pope to our cause, nor to make him a neophyte to our principles, or a propagator of our ideas. Such would be an insane dream. That which we should seek, that which we should await, as the Jews await a Messiah, is a Pope according to our wants...We require a Pope for ourselves, if such a Pope were possible. With such a one we should march more securely to the storming of the Church than with all the little books of our French and English brothers. And why? Because it were useless to seek with these alone to split the rock upon which God has built his Church. We should not want the vinegar of Hannibal, nor gunpowder, nor even our arms, if we had but the little finger of the successor of Peter engaged in the plot. We trust that we may yet attain this supreme object of our efforts."

Is the statement of the Alta Vendita real or is it all too pat? We may never know. What we do know is that sentiments like those expressed in the document were rife throughout Europe. If the Alta Vendita was a hoax it was a hoax possessed of a remarkable verisimilitude.[2]

Rome and the OTO

Whether or not the Alta Vendita is mere legend or something more, it is certainly consonant with the documentary record concerning occult infiltration of the

---

[2] The best argument in favor of the authenticity of the Alta Vendita document has been made by the gifted Catholic journalist John Vennari in *The Permanent Instruction of the Alta Vendita*.

Church. One part of that record concerns the OTO's successful recruitment of a powerful Cardinal, already a Freemason, into its ranks, none other than the Vatican Secretary of State, Mariano Cardinal Rampolla, second only to the Pope in power. This fact can be verified by accessing the list of elite members contained in the *1917 Manifesto of the OTO*, a list which included the name of Cardinal Rampolla. The irony is that Rampolla worked in the pontificate of Leo XIII, the Pope who had penned the most scathing Encyclical against Freemasonry ever issued.

After the death of this pope, the Cardinals formed a Conclave to elect his successor. The easy victory fell, by sheer weight of votes, to Cardinal Rampolla. It now appeared that a Freemason and OTO Satanist was about to be named pope. Imagine the jubilation back in the chambers of Theodor Reuss with his OTO minions. But enter Monsignor Ernest Jouin, an alert investigator of secret societies. He had learned that Rampolla was secretly a Freemason; Jouin also had foreseen the direction of the Papal Conclave. In response, Jouin persuaded Emperor Franz Josef of Austria-Hungary to invoke the seventeenth century "Right of Exclusion," a long forgotten clause in a treaty between Vienna and the Vatican. This treaty gave Franz Josef the power to veto the election of a pope. The Conclave was stunned when Cardinal Puzyna, the Metropolitan of Krakow, rose to his feet and pronounced a veto of the election of Rampolla, under the terms of this treaty.

Once the facts about him were verified, Rampolla was finished. The treaty was in force, and the Right of Exclusion could not be denied. After the smoke cleared, the Conclave recast, electing Giuseppe Cardinal Sarto, who became Pope Pius X. After Rampolla's death, the facts emerged that confirmed his membership in the OTO. Pius X is said to have commented, "Miserable man!"

But Rampolla's role was not necessarily completely thwarted by his failure to ascend to the Papacy. Even with Pius X, a dedicated and holy man, in power, Rampolla influenced key men who were to shape the Papacy in the 20th Century. Giacomo Della Chiesa, later Benedict XV, was chosen by Rampolla to be his private secretary at the Nunciature in Madrid. Rampolla also brought Pietro Gasparri from the Catholic Institute in Paris to Rome as his chief assistant, and Gasparri is said to have had influence during the reign of Pius XI. Eugenio Cardinal Pacelli, the future Pius XII, was private secretary to

Rampolla. Angelo Roncalli, the future John XXIII, was assisted by Rampolla's good friend and confidant, Msgr. Radini-Tedeschi. Roncalli became the latter's private secretary. The father of Giovanni Cardinal Montini, later Paul VI, caught Rampolla's fancy with his idea of a Church-sponsored political party. Through Rampolla, the Secretary of State, the OTO had the opportunity to give counsel, plant seeds and ultimately shape policy within the Vatican. [3]

Let us examine one of these prelates, the much-esteemed Eugenio Pacelli (Pius XII). Pacelli, sad to say, did seem to reflect lines of OTO influence. He agreed to the suppression of the immensely popular American "radio priest," Fr. Charles Coughlin, for advocating peace with Germany, speaking truthfully about Franklin Roosevelt's war mongering, and exposing malevolent Judaic influence over the U.S. government, economics and entertainment.

In spite of the fact that he and his intelligence apparatus should have known that the United Nations was a Masonic project (the League of Nations was well-known to the Vatican as Masonic), Pacelli endorsed the UN and appointed Roncalli as the Vatican's first United Nations "observer." Pacelli, during his tenure as Pope Pius XII declared:

"Although the United Nations' condemnation of the grave violations of the rights of men and of entire nations is worthy of recognition, one may nevertheless wish that, in similar cases, the exercise of their rights, as members of this organization, be denied to States which refuse even the admission of observers--thus showing that their concept of State sovereignty threatens the very foundations of the United Nations.

"This organization ought also to have the right and the power of forestalling all military intervention of one State in another, whatever the pretext under which it is effected, and also the right and power of assuming, by means of a sufficient police force, the safeguarding of order in the State which is threatened. "If we allude to these defects, it is because we desire to see the authority of the United Nations strengthened, especially for effecting general disarmament, which we have so much at heart. In fact, only in the ambitions of an institution such as the U.N.

---

[3] I'm only suggesting gradual positioning and infiltration and influence here--getting men in place like the early stages of a chess game. The middle game is where the action happens, and for modern times that was Vatican II and the post-Conciliar era.

can the promise of individual nations to reduce armaments, especially to abandon production and use of certain weapons, be mutually exchanged under the strict obligation of international law...Likewise only the United Nations is at present in a position to exact the observance of this obligation by assuming effective control of the armaments of all nations without exception." [4]

Pacelli/Pius XII chose Bugnini, the scalawag who would later play a major role in the tyrannical suppression of the Tridentine Mass, to "reform" the Holy Week liturgy. Without this pivotal promotion, Bugnini would probably never have been in line to do a hatchet job on the Mass.

Aleister Crowley's obsession with the Roman Catholic Mass and his desire to create a Gnostic Mass for the OTO can be viewed against this particular backdrop. The OTO has a love-hate relationship with the Catholic Church, hating it for holding up to the world Jesus Christ Crucified, but envying its power and grandeur and hoping to infect with it a Thelemic stamp, as had been attempted centuries earlier by "Christian Kabbalists" such as Pico della Mirandola and Johannes Reuchlin, whose infiltration was given a head-wound by the Council of Trent.

OTO magus Kenneth Grant has rhapsodized about "the Energy of Satan that will permeate the earth during the present cycle." [5]

As the duped kabbalistic "limbs of Satan," many Thelemites are positioning themselves with the secrecy of a British spy and the zeal of an inverted Billy Graham in order to subvert the Church and spread the gospel of Crowleyanity. That signifies that they are aware that the enormous institution that is the Catholic Church must either become gnostic or be rendered harmless and impotent. The Roman Catholic Church has indeed undergone startling changes since the days of of Rampolla and his Vatican "academy," and they are worthy of comment. The upheaval in the Church which followed the Second Vatican Council, ("Vatican II," 1963-65), left many older Catholics utterly bewildered, and for good reason. While many statements made at the Council appeared to be traditional and filled with a Christian spirit, a few faithful Vatican insiders such as Dietrich von Hildebrand

---

[4] Transcript of his radio broadcast of December 23, 1956, in *The Pope Speaks: The Teachings of Pope Pius XII.* New York: Pantheon, 1957, p. 328.

[5] *Aleister Crowley and the Hidden God,* p. 60.

and Alfredo Cardinal Ottaviani, began to warn of a Fifth Column which had successfully infiltrated Rome, a "Trojan horse in the City of God."

Investigators of Freemasonry and the occult need register no surprise, knowing that efforts to get a Gnostic foothold in the Church go back to the attempt by Valentinus, the early Gnostic leader, to be pope, and various popes such as Alexander VI and Sixtus V have favored occult schemers.

The OTO actually celebrated the opening of the Second Vatican Council. Just three weeks before the death of OTO leader Karl Germer on October 11, 1962, Vatican II commenced, while simultaneously the OTO conducted its own ritual intended to influence the outcome of the Council. It was based on Crowley's obsession with the "Stele of Revealing" which in 1904 had inspired his (then) wife Rose--who showed it to Crowley in the Boulak Museum in Cairo, Egypt--to persuade him to wait on "spirits," which he did for three days, emerging with his *Book of the Law.* [6]

Hermann Metzger reported in *Oriflamme* that "during the opening of the Second Vatican Ecumenical Council, the Stele of Revealing was carried across Germany from Hamburg to Zurich, and thence to Stein, where it was borne into the Chapel while all the bells were ringing."

The Smoke of Satan

The Catholic Church was in part given a new charter at this Council, and began increasingly to serve the purposes of rabbis in the most obvious and even absurd manner. This inversion emerged officially with the 1965 Vatican II document, *Nostra Aetate* ("In Our Time"), in which 2000 years of Biblical truth was reversed in a declaration that stated Jews did not kill Christ, even though the Bible declares otherwise (I Thessalonians 2:14-15) and the Talmud actually boasts of this decide (Sanhedrin 43a). No matter, times had changed and "in our time" signaled Rome's embrace of the temporal chauvinism of the modern age, and the foretold march of masonic decay. *Nostra Aetate* removed a traditional Catholic adversarial perception of Judaism and cleared the way for a gradual transformation of the Church at the

---

[6] Friedrich Levke possessed a printing plate of the Stele, identical with the plate used by Crowley in the volumes of his journal *Equinox.*

hands of the now sought-after rabbis. Like the OTO, the Catholic Church made these changes under a pretense of liberty and progress. Like the OTO, dissent from this agenda was crushed, and like the OTO, inversions of appearance and reality abound. The Gnostic Catholic and Roman Catholic Churches have actually achieved a measure of convergence.

Other changes following Vatican II were also of occult provenance. For example, demands for female priests--the Gnostic Mass has had priestesses for close to a century. Anglicans and Lutherans are already "ahead" in this area. The Council documents, once used to open a door, were actually afterward largely ignored; the tactic of the rebels was, so to speak, not of the documents of Vatican II, but rather of the "spirit of Vatican II," which, remaining nebulous and undefined, allowed for any innovation which gained a following. "Ecumenism," previously an attempt to re-gather separated Christians into the Catholic fold, devolved into a syncretism indistinguishable from classic Masonic brotherhood doctrine, including tolerance for Voodoo in Benin, Africa. The post-Vatican II Church took care to not violate anyone's "True Will."

Rampolla had sought to gain a pope for the OTO; Crowley devised a Gnostic Mass and Pike's prophesy was fulfilled when Thelema got not one, but three of their own on the Chair of Peter, "the Johns and the Pauls," (John XXIII, Paul VI and John-Paul II). [7]

Attempts by the Left-playing wing of the OTO to undermine the Church had not ended with Cardinal Rampolla. Archbishop Annibale Bugnini, whose name appeared with many other prominent Vatican prelates on a list of Freemasons seized by police from an Italian Masonic Lodge in 1976, presided over the creation in 1969 of the *Novus Ordo Missae* (New Order Mass), which, although capable of reverence when performed in Latin, tended to descend to liturgical banality, if not absurdity, in

---

[7] The short-lived Pope John Paul I (Albino Luciani, 1912-1978), who reigned for just *33* days, is largely an enigma, with his untimely death rumored to have been an assassination. Cf. David Yallop, *In God's Name: An Investigation into the Murder of Pope John Paul I* (Corgi, 1997). The suggestion that he was killed because he intended to restore the Church to its pre-Vatican II status is not sustained by the available evidence. For background on other potential murderers and motives involving the Vatican Bank and the P-2 Lodge, cf. Nick Tosches, *Power on Earth* (Arbor House, 1986).

the translation and typical adaptation in the average
Catholic parish, if not outright heresy, sparking a
revolution that emptied pews, convents and seminaries
and prompted Paul VI to blurt in an unguarded moment,
"the smoke of Satan has entered the Church." [8]

Bugnini may not have been in the OTO, but as a
Freemason he succeeded in helping to replace the
Tridentine Mass with a liturgy that evolved, after 1969,
into something vaguely Masonic. It may not be the Gnostic
Mass of the OTO, but in its abused form, it is undeniably a
step closer to it. Some say that the trouble with the *Novus
Ordo* and the culture that accompanied its promulgation,
was not necessarily with the original, official, 1969 Latin
version of this Mass authorized by Paul VI--though this is
hotly disputed--but in the degree to which Bugnini was
able to implement and exploit, in its wake, a culture of
desacrilization and irreverence; of "anything goes"
experimentation and innovation-for-innovation's-sake,
that led to institutionalized ruin.

A significant fact concerning the liturgy of the post-
Vatican II Church is that leading Catholic prelates have
indirectly espoused Crowley's perspective on "worship," so
that when they speak of "the Faith" we must ask, *faith in
whom*, the Lord or Lucifer? [9]

The Charismatic "speaking in tongues" movement,
once listed as a sign of Demonic Possession in the old
Roman Ritual of Exorcism, was vigorously championed by
Joseph Cardinal Suenens, whose name also appeared on

---

[8] Either that, or Paul VI was playing a chess game with the
faithful by posing as a confused bystander in the devil's
smokehouse, when it was he who had built the house. The *Novus
Ordo* Mass was promulgated not long after the encyclical
Humanae Vitae, Paul VI's powerful reaffirmation of the Apostolic
teaching on contraception and abortion, prompting naive
Catholic Conservatives to accept the *Novus Ordo* Mass on the
basis of the Pope's orthodoxy in *Humanae Vitae*. In this case,
Lenin's dictum may apply: "Two steps forward, one step back."

[9] Some learned Catholics argue forcefully that the *Novus Ordo
Missae* is defective even in its original essence as promulgated by
Paul VI, and that the Tridentine Mass is the only reliable
liturgical sanctuary. Others say that this line of attack calls into
question papal infallibility and that the problem rests entirely
with "abuses" of the Novus Ordo that have evolved over the
years. This latter faction believes that in exercising his
"magisterial" teaching function (*lex orandi, lex credendi*), Paul VI
could not promulgate a defective liturgy.

the aforementioned membership roster of the Italian Masonic Lodge. Some modern Catholic Charismatic "happenings" have whipped up such stimulation that the frenzied hysteria of the crowd very thinly covers their erotic arousal with a mask of religiosity, if it is covered at all. The revision of witchcraft known as Wicca—an OTO encampment, as we saw earlier—is running rampant in the Catholic Women's Movement and even in nuns' convents.

Solve et Coagula

The Left wing of the OTO was breaking the Church down, in part so that the Right wing of the OTO could rebuild it, by assuming control, behind the scenes, of the anticipated backlash from the traditionalist survivors of the Left-wing purge. The OTO, as described in chapter three, is shaping the Right wing reaction by putting their agents in place within the leadership of certain priestly fraternities pledged to restore the old ways.

As part of the Left-wing campaign of dissolution, doctrinally precise catechisms were discarded and replaced with vague, vapid, feel-good books and insipid ditties. Practicing a demanding teaching or striving for a difficult sanctity has been replaced with the equivalent of the occult "assumption of the godform" which Crowley taught in his other, allied kabbalistic Order, the *Argenteum Astrum*—the practice of visualizing being clothed as a deity. Modernist Catholics find it easier to smile and picture being vaguely clothed with Jesus than trying to follow Him to a personal cross in which self-centeredness and illusion are put to death.

Classic Catholic art and architecture were replaced with dangling banners sporting trite sayings similar to those of Tony Robbins, Norman Vincent Peale or Yoda from Star Wars, and sterile modern art. One overt signal of occult infiltration in the Catholic Church came through a painting. In 1970 a German Lutheran received permission from Pope Paul VI to observe him during papal audiences in order to paint his portrait. Ernst Günter Hansing presented the Pope with the finished portrait in 1972. It was published in full color in the April 1972 edition of the Smithsonian, together with Paul VI's cryptic commentary: the Pope stated that the portrait is "a mirror of the situation in the Church today," and furthermore that "one almost needs a new philosophy to grasp the meaning of this in its context."

The last comment is certainly no understatement, for

the painting is pure Revelation-of-the-Method and portrays the pontiff as not merely ugly, but even repellent and evil-- clutching a dagger and destroying St. Peter's Basilica. The Masonic square and compass is clearly discernible above him, as well as the traditional "point within the circle," symbol of Weishaupt's Illuminati. The portrait also contains an abstract Eye in a Triangle—known as the Eye of Set or Sirius. Several inverted crosses—typical symbols of Satanism—are also discernible.

The Pope's ambiguity concerning the diabolic images themes in the painting and his public acceptance of the portrait and its artist appear to be signals for those who could discern their meaning. For the rest, the painting produced in percipients a deepening of the tragic schizophrenia with which modern Catholics have been afflicted as they have been swept into the New Aeon. Paul VI seems, however, to see things as they are in this picture. He is quite clear. He understood that it reflected, as in a mirror, the events in the Church as they truly were happening. He understood that the key to grasping the meaning of the painting is a new philosophy—the philosophy of Thelema—which in turn enables us to grasp the portrait in its context—a context which is the Aeon of Horus.

Decades later, the year 2000 brought the Catholic world a truly grotesque sight. In the middle of the supposed Millennium, the elderly, decrepit Pope John Paul II visited "Israel," and was publicly seated across from a rabbi, in a chair with an inverted cross, the main symbol of Satanism, looming across the backrest. While St. Peter is said to have been crucified upside-down, it is also true that an upside-down cross is not part of any Catholic iconography. The symbolism and meaning of the inverted cross in Satanism are well known. The grinning rabbi across from the Pope completed the surreal moment.

The list of scandals is interminable. Objective observers can see that the Roman Catholic Church, long an obsession of Freemasonry, has been vigorously kicked in the shins. But one can go further: the Roman Catholic Church shows signs of Thelemization. It shows the assimilation of concepts and practices from the Left-wing of the OTO, holes in the Barque of Peter which betray the presence of termites from the Cult of the Beast. It appears that under the aegis of *Aggiornamento* (or "updating"), the slogan of Pope John XXIII, the major portion of the Roman

Catholic Church has been moved toward a greater convergence with the OTO's Leftist wing. Is it any wonder the OTO celebrated when Vatican II opened? The post-Conciliar Church also opened itself to homosexual seminarians and clergymen and to a non-confrontational approach toward Freemasonry, to the glee of the conspirators who still bitterly recalled the era of popes from Gregory XVI to Leo XIII, and especially the pontificate of Pope St. Pius X, who were all strongly anti-Masonic and renewed multiple times the decree of excommunication for all Freemasons, a decree which was modified significantly by Pope John Paul II in 1983. [10]

Baphomet Baptists

The abiding interest of the Gnostic Catholic Church in the Roman Catholic leads to the natural question about the place of the Protestants in the Thelemic landscape. This question carries an ironic dimension, because if the question were reversed, certain Protestants would be quick to speak about the OTO, a subject which exerts a fascination with some of them. Indeed, there exists a group of fanatical but sincere Fundamentalists who are obsessed with Aleister Crowley, lapping up tidbits about him in order to expose him as the true father of all things Satanic and dark in the world—that is, if they are not busy exposing the procession of popes as such. The problem here however, is the myopia of the Protestants involved, who fail to examine the role Protestantism has played in empowering the Thelemic occult current. They tend to view the Catholics as entirely culpable in this vein while absolving the founders of the Protestant Church of any responsibility.

There is even one ex-OTO-Satanist-Mason-Witch-Mormon-turned-Protestant writer (published by the anti-Catholic propagandist Jack Chick) who is convinced that the penetration of the Gnostic Catholic Church in the Roman is an indication that the Protestant churches are the pure and simple truth. (Of course this fellow is a Zionist).

---

[10] As one indication of the dramatic reversal, Paulist Press—the largest Catholic publisher—has produced several sanitized and abridged editions of the Talmud, the Zohar, and other kabbalistic texts and rabbinical fairy tales. Such attempts under the pontificate of St. Pius X would likely have incurred swift excommunication.

We should recall that Aleister Crowley was the son of a Protestant minister of the strict Plymouth Brethren sect. Nor is it very strange that one of the most important leaders of the OTO, Michael Bertiaux, leader of the OTOA (*Ordo Templi Orientis Antiqua*), was ordained an Episcopalian priest.

Just as the son of Rabbi Judes Lion Bimstein lay in the shadows behind the kabbalistic origin of the OTO, so the spirit of the Reformation was in part shaped by rabbis and Rosicrucians who hoped to loosen the heavy Roman Catholic grip and allow a greater freedom to the underground Gnostics and necromancers.

Martin Luther's connection with hidden masters in his early career is the lore of occult circles. Luther's personal seal was the Rose Cross, although this fact does not prove that Luther was a conscious agent of Rosicrucians. Johann Andrea, an early Lutheran clergyman, had strong ties to Rosicrucianism.

With rabbis and Rosicrucians helping out in the background, Protestantism quickly found a royal "marriage" in England between throne and theurgy. Dr. John Dee (1527-1608), Royal Astrologer to Elizabeth I, worked with trance-medium Sir Edward Kelley (1555-1595) to create a system of occult invocations to demons which he styled The Enochian Calls. This system remains to this day a profound influence upon the magick of the Great Beast 666 and his Argenteum Astrum, Silver Star Order. It is from the Enochian system of Dee that Crowley derived the spelling of the title of his Scarlet Woman, the woman of blood, "Babalon."

Dee, a member of the Anglican church, was the original "007," the cipher being Dee's code for signing confidential communications. Ian Fleming, author of the modern James Bond stories featuring 007, was, like fellow agent Aleister Crowley, a member of British Intelligence.

Michael A. Hoffman II points out that Dee was the architect of the very concept of "British Empire" and "British Israel." Hoffman claims that Dee fused devotion to Judaism with the material advance of the fortunes of Protestant empire in laying the groundwork for the rise of British Freemasonry. Hence, Freemasonry was always strongly Anglican in character, and a great many Anglican aristocrats, clergymen and government officials--in addition to the monarchs themselves--were Freemasons.

So steeped in the occult was the Anglican Church that as part of its thinly veiled goddess worship, Anglicans appointed a woman (Queen Elizabeth I) as head of the Church. Protestants who criticize all Catholic devotion to the Blessed Virgin Mary as a revival of pagan goddess cultism, overlook the fact that Elizabeth, in her revolutionary role as the female head of the Church of England, was regarded by Renaissance occultists as the new Isis. This adoration was presented allegorically in Sir Edmund Spenser's renowned poetic epic, *The Faerie Queen*. [11]

The mainline Southern Baptist Church is no less tainted, being rife with Freemasons. In 1993, after nearly a year-long study, the Home Missions Board of the Southern Baptist Interfaith Witness Department, rejected the allegation that Freemasonry is incompatible with Christianity and Southern Baptist teaching. This ruling was a triumph for countless Baptist Masons, all of whom no doubt thanked the Great Architect.

Methodism does not differ notably in this respect, either. The experience of the Reverend Harmon Taylor, a Methodist pastor, is typical. In his words, he became a Freemason, "When I looked out in the congregation, (and saw that) there were Masonic lapel pins on all but one of the men." Protestant writer Ed Decker recounts his early experience lecturing on his former Mormon beliefs before a Protestant congregation. Recounting the Mormon Temple rituals in intimate detail, he was angrily approached afterward by church elders, who allegedly told him to stop his exposure or he would get hurt. They told him that in revealing the secrets of Mormonism he was revealing Masonic secrets.

Decker defiantly informed these crypto-Masons that he would commence an investigation of Freemasonry next, since if it was the same thing as Mormonism, then it had to come from the "same pit of Hell." Decker eventually discovered that Joseph Smith, the serial adulterer who founded the Mormon Church, was a Master Mason whose Temple rituals were "borrowed" from Masonic lodges. Smith was murdered by a masonic mob in Illinois in 1844, for breaking his Masonic blood oaths and revealing their secrets. Initiated Mormons today are told that they have the "true Masonry."

Norman Vincent Peale, the popular Protestant preacher of "positive thinking," was a prominent 33rd degree Freemason. The OTO's James Wasserman writes, "The rise and survival of the Protestant movement

[11] Cf. in particular *Faerie Queen* Book V, Canto vii.

demonstrated beyond argument the weakened state of the Church, and the loss of its hitherto unchallenged thousand-year monopoly on the religious life of Europe." [12]

Protestants need to be reminded, particularly the anti-Catholics among them, that denunciations of Freemasonry and the occult ring hollow if they do not also denounce the Judeo-masonic influence over certain Protestant founders and denominations. Protestants who adopt a tone of superiority regarding Thelemic successes within Catholicism should be reminded that while the Goat of Mendes has been galloping through Catholic churches, Baphomet has been playing the Baptist organ, and preaching to the Anglican choir.

---

[12] *The Templars and the Assassins: The Militia of Heaven*, p. 256.

IX

Politics and Pedophilia

"Come forth, o children, under the stars, and take your fill of love!"

Recent revelations of pederasty involving Catholic priests highlight another convergence, the Church has been remade in the image and likeness of the Gnostic. But this fact lies buried beneath the histrionics and outrage at clerical homosexuality from the very media pundits who have tirelessly promoted sodomy and ethical relativism. Their placid hypocrisy is part of the intended mass hypnosis; a mystical charade to test the trance-state of the populace and adjust their programming based on our response.

The cozy beneath-the-sheets relationship of the media, the OTO, political cover-up and pedophilia is typified by the English journalist Walter Duranty, the Pulitzer Prize-winning "Man in Moscow" for the *New York Times*. While Soviet dictator Josef Stalin was inflicting genocide upon the Ukrainian Kulak farmers in 1932-33, a crime exposed in reports by Malcolm Muggeridge, Walter Duranty was busy writing as the *Times* Moscow correspondent that all such stories were lies. In a March 31, 1933 report, Duranty derided accounts of Stalin's imposed famine against the peasants as "mostly bunk," holding that "there is no actual starvation or deaths from starvation...."

Duranty was awarded the Pulitzer Prize in 1933 for his "scholarship, profundity, impartiality, sound judgment, and exceptional clarity." Following this award, Franklin Roosevelt extended his hand to Stalin, the Communist murderer of Christians and offered diplomatic recognition to the USSR.

The facts about Duranty himself, like the truth behind his lies, provide an even stranger contrast to his public image. In 1914, Aleister Crowley embarked upon the "Paris Working," a series of twenty-four sexual rituals spread over seven weeks. The first ritual occurred on New Year's Eve, 1914 in the late afternoon, in which Crowley "confessed" himself and, according to his notes, received "the Sacrament (sex) from a certain priest A.B." A.B. was Walter Duranty, code-named "Art-Bachelor Gualterius de R., Universitatis Cantabrigiensis."

Duranty and Crowley had been carrying on in such a manner, minus the "festive" rituals, for some time. They also drew into their circle Jane Chéron, later Duranty's wife. The nature of these rituals can be glimpsed through a few examples. Working up to midnight of the New Year, Crowley chased a naked Orthodox Jewish poet, Victor Neuburg, ritually scourging his buttocks with sufficient force to draw blood. At midnight, Crowley and Neuburg engaged in sodomy, reciting a verse in Latin composed by Duranty and Crowley, supposedly calculated to invoke the god Mercury. The result was that Neuburg began babbling as though he believed himself to be the mouthpiece of Mercury, and Crowley took everything babbled quite literally. On January 3 1914, during the Third Working, "Mercury" instructed Crowley to perform "an holy act before the world." Crowley's interpretation was to engage in sodomy with Neuburg in front of the future Mrs. Duranty.

The Beast and his priest composed several Latin "holy hymns" for use during the Paris Working (in reality these consisted of smutty and pathetic doggerel). The pederastic imagery of these "hymns", like Duranty's pro-Communist prevarication, is no Astrum accident. In his *Commentary on The Book of the Law,* the bisexual Crowley writes of the need to freak freely, drawing a parallel between old-fashioned discretion in sexual matters and the new morality of "courageous Thelemic candor" whereby men proudly behave like beasts. Crowley argues that "Incest, Adultery, and Pæderstasty" should be openly practiced without "shame, slyness, cowardice" or "hypocrisy." Crowley demanded nothing less than childhood's end: "...the Beast 666 adviseth that all children shall be accustomed from infancy to witness every type of sexual act..." His advice has been taken to heart by the Hollywood entertainment industry and the New York publishing houses, consonant with the supreme status that homosexual anal intercourse exerts as the highest rite in the OTO: the 11th degree, code-named "the Eye within the

Triangle," or "Eye of Set." [1]

The successors of Duranty stare at us in suits and make-up from large TV screens, reading their lines with the studied inflections and eyebrow shifts of mock earnestness. The increasing adoption in society at large of the OTO's Gnostic-Thelemic "ethic"—these facts you will not read in the *New York Times*.

Child Molestation in the Talmud

The roots of these pedophiliac practices, however, are not the Great Beast himself, nor even the OTO. The Cult of the Beast is an important modern branch from a much older tree. We must look back, past the incomplete initiation given to occultists through the centuries by their tutors and masters, to discern the roots of institutionalized sodomy of children. These roots are not in *The Book of the Law*, which may almost be considered an abridgment of something much older. The roots of pedophilia, at least as far as the West is concerned, lie in the secrets of the Talmud. This provocative statement is not difficult to verify today, thanks to the accurate translation of a partial edition of the Talmud in English translated by Adin Steinsaltz. [2]

In Ketubot 11b, for example, we read "If a grown man has intercourse with a little girl less than three years old, all agree that it is not considered a significant sexual act, for having intercourse with a girl when she is less than three years old is like putting a finger in an eye." This is but one verified example of many rabbinical sanctions of child molestation and pedophilia. The Steinsaltz edition quotes, as background, a principle from the *Halakhah* (Judaism's man-made laws): "There is a Halakhic principle that sexual intercourse with a girl less than three years and one day old is not considered intercourse at all...genital contact below a certain age cannot be considered sexual activity."

This loophole legalism is quintessentially Talmudic, for

---

[1] Aleister Crowley, *The Law is for All*, pp. 54-55.

[2] Publication of the Steinsaltz Talmud in English was interrupted by Random House after only the first 21 volumes were printed, for reasons that have never been made clear.

the Talmud is the font of legal shysterism and a basis of the ethics of the OTO's kabbalistic Right-wing "pillar."

It was easier to speak openly of these matters decades ago than it is now. A giant of American letters like H. L. Mencken was free to opine, "I am one of the few Goyim who have ever actually tackled the Talmud. I suppose you now expect me to add that it is a profound and noble work, worthy of hard study by all other Goyim. Unhappily, my report must differ from this expectation. It seems to me, save for a few bright spots, to be quite indistinguishable from rubbish." [3]

Sanhedrin is a portion of the Talmud named after the rabbinic tribunal which sentenced Christ to death. In Sanhedrin 54b we read this argument: "...whoever can perpetrate sodomy can also be the object of sodomy. And whoever cannot perpetrate sodomy can also not be the object of sodomy. If a boy under the age of nine perpetrated sodomy upon an adult, the adult is not liable for punishment, for the intercourse of a boy under nine years of age is not legally an act of intercourse. Since a child less than nine years old cannot commit sodomy, he can also not be the object of sodomy." Such lawyerly knavery is nothing less than permission for homosexual pederasty. Judaic *Halakha* even offers absolution for accidental (!) sodomy: "If a man unwittingly perpetrated sodomy upon another man, and also allowed himself to be the object of sodomy with another man, all in a single 'period of unawareness,' he is only liable for a single sin-offering."

A ritual such as the Paris Working successfully invokes a state of trance, hence, we now know why the orthodox "Jew" Victor Neuburg engaged in these acts with Crowley: in a trance-state, he was in a "period of unawareness," and his homosexual acts were not culpable in the eyes of the rabbis, except as a kind of minor lapse in discretion.

Sodomy in the synagogue is a well-kept secret. A code of silence blankets this topic, which could easily receive front-page press, if the press in the United States were truly free. The Hebrew language Israeli newspaper *Ha'aretz* reported on February 1, 2000, that decades of

---

[3] Quoted by William N. Grimstad, *AntiZion*. Noontide Press, 1985.

sodomizing of yeshiva (all-male Talmud school) students was permitted and covered up by "the greatest of the ultra-Orthodox rabbis...like Rabbi Landau and the halachic sage Shmuel Halevi Hausner of Bnei Brak..." [4]

The Talmud derives its mentality mainly from older occult lineages and kingdoms of pagan priestcraft, including Egypt and Babylon, all important sources for the OTO. In turn, these civilizations can be said to be extended developments of the perspective of the serpent in Genesis who taught Adam and Eve to be "as gods" and Do What They Wilt. Crowley claims Satan as the "initiator" who "made Gods of our race..." The Israelites of yore did not resist the siren call of Egypt, and danced around the Golden Calf and carried occult Egypt in their hearts. Rabbis mimicked the Pharaonic priestcraft and the ultimate product was the Mishnah and Gemara, the black magical essence of which is the Kabbalah.

Thus, in the midst of Christendom, a petrie dish of abominable pagan superstition was passed down. While the Great Beast's Book of the Law enshrined relativized Talmudic perspectives within the official higher levels of the Masonic Academy known as the OTO, the Talmud with its Right-wing emphasis on the rabbis as nit-picking lawyers, was not usually quoted directly to the lower ranks, but rather the Kabbalah, with its Left-wing emphasis on the rabbis as Merlinesque mystic masters possessing the blueprint of infinite creation, was openly acknowledged. Crowley testifies, "The whole basis of our theory is the Qabalah....The Holy Qabalah, based as it is on pure number, evidently possesses an infinite number of symbols. Its scope is co-terminous with existence itself, and it lacks nothing in precision, purity, or indeed in any other perfection. The Qabalah is therefore a living Temple of the Holy Ghost...In the light of the Qabalah, the shadows of transitory things are instantly banished." [5]

Crowley's view is nearly identical to the teachings of "Palladium" Pike in this context, who writes "Masonry is a search after Light. That search leads us directly back, as

---

[4] Quoted in Hoffman, *Judaism's Strange Gods*, pp. 76-79.

[5] *Magic in Theory and Practice*. Cf. pp. 143; 252-253; 277.

you see, to the Kabbalah." [6]

Judaism's foundational role as the basis for the OTO's Cult of the Beast is little known. Thanks to the "Holy Kabbalah" and the rationalizers of pedophilia who wrote the Talmud, pedophilia had an existing, secret base from which to propagandize our culture, and certain Crowley-connected players began to do so with aggressive zeal.

It should be noted that this writer is in no way claiming or even implying that every OTO member is necessarily a pedophile. Many in the OTO are no doubt opposed to pedophilia, though on what grounds it would be difficult to say, given the license Crowley bestowed upon virtually every imaginable form of what until recently, was diagnosed by physicians as clinically insane perversion.

One of the first to lift the onus of psychiatric stigma was the Thelemic sexual liberator Dr. Alfred Kinsey, who was recently exposed as a pedophile himself. Much of Kinsey's "research" involved children. Kinsey was so enamored with the Beast that he made a pilgrimage to Crowley's Abbey of Thelema in Cefalù, Sicily, to pay tribute to his idol. The doctor even tried to acquire the "Magical Diaries" of Crowley for the Kinsey Institute, a telling indication of the "scientific" basis of Kinsey's "discoveries." [7]

Another OTO "gay" rights advocate was Communist Party activist Harry Hay, who played the organ at the Gnostic Mass in the Los Angeles Agape Lodge. Hay founded the Mattachine Society, a pioneering homosexual rights' lobby. When NAMBLA, (the North American Man/Boy Love Association), was denied a role in the 1986 Los Angeles "Gay" Pride Parade, Hay marched defiantly with a sweatshirt sporting the message, "NAMBLA Walks With Me." Crowley regarded any separation between homosexuality and pederasty as artificial and absurd and refused to restrict himself. As it says in *The Book of the Law*, "the word of Sin is Restriction." (1:41)

The Gay Lesbian Straight Education Network (GLSEN) of Boston, Massachusetts hosted a party on November 17-19, 2000, advertised as "A Return to the Chicken Ranch." In the argot of pedophiles, very young sex partners are

---

[6] *Morals and Dogma,* p. 741.

[7] Cf. Judith Reisman, *Kinsey: Crimes and Consequences.*

known collectively as "chickens." GLSEN successfully promotes "Tolerance Clubs" (the "Gay-Straight Alliance" or GSA) in schools nationwide.

Recent developments in this "tolerance crusade" include coining the designation "LGTB" or "Lesbian-Gay-Transgendered-Bisexual" and referring to men who have had themselves castrated as "she, Madam" and "Miss." These pitiable victims of test-tube hormones and modern plastic surgery cannot lactate, menstruate, or become pregnant, yet it is now a virtual hate crime in some American cities to refer to these tragic persons as sir, mister or anything other than "women."

The sanctioning legislation, judicial rulings and fad-like, chic popularity of these "crimes against nature" in the US and Europe, have resulted in nature (and reality itself) being outlawed, a fact which environmental groups overlook in their campaign on behalf of nature.

Rights for the *transgendered* have become a staple of a *transformed* America on the part of occult puppet-masters in the media and government who seek to impose these "liberating lifestyle" and cultural "initiatives" on the Muslim world. When Muslims resist, they are castigated as backward, medieval oppressors stuck in a retrograde moral and educational condition. Yet, many of these "initiatives," in spite of Republican cant about "family values," carry within them the seeds of Thelema. [8]

The "Sin of Restriction" is now viewed by influential American educators, journalists and judges precisely as Crowley viewed it, a century ago. What of the rest of his far-sighted agenda? Soon to be seen: the "right" to engage in bestiality and necrophilia. Is it a victimless crime if the sheep is willing? Can a lifeless corpse be a "legal" victim? Don't be surprised to see these arguments promoted in the Talmudic-Thelemic cauldron that is the U.S.A.

---

[8] The "transgendered" "lifestyle" is promoted on the Right where "market forces" and unbridled capitalism are embraced. The Holiday 2004 *Booklist and Review* (p. 31) of "Laissez Faire Books," promotes *Crossing,* a book they advertise as a "memoir" of an economist who "...chose to resolve his personal conflicts by becoming a woman." Moreover, the practice of sodomy is not confined to men. Toni Bentley is the author of a celebrated paean to sodomy, *The Surrender*. Ms. Bentley calls anal sex "bliss..the direct path...to God." (*NY Times*, Oct. 15, 2004, pp. B-27 & B-32).

X

Panpipes to a Still-Born Aeon

"For I have crushed an Universe; & nought remains."

This book would not be complete without exhibiting some of the most important symptoms of the success of the OTO's long-projected planetary initiation. Much like a lingering vampire still occasionally feeding from the neck of a hypnotized populace, Crowley has triumphed to no small degree, since currently the Goyim are practically slumbering, blood-drained, in the arms of their Overlords.

Some OTO successes have been due to political influences, as we have seen in earlier chapters. Typical of Crowley's efforts in this area was his recruitment of Major-General John Frederick Charles Fuller (1878-1966), the famed British military officer and strategist, as his Second-in-Command in the Order of the Silver Star (AA). Fuller invented the Blitzkrieg tactic, ignored by the British, but adopted by Hitler's army. Less well-known is another invention of Fuller's: the term "Crowleyanity." With Fuller under his belt (for a time), Crowley was able to boast that "a certain brother...is in the most secret of England's War Councils at this hour." Later Fuller would maintain a diplomatic distance from the Beast.

More success for the Beast was to come in the crucial domain of composing a nation's myths, the modern arts of science and science fiction. Honored scientist John Whiteside Parsons was the OTO leader of the Agape Lodge in California. He was the inventor of jet-assisted takeoff (JATO), the founder of Aerojet Corporation and the co-founder of the Jet Propulsion Laboratory (JPL). [1]

Author of instrumental research behind both our space program and Allied military victories during World War II, Parsons (known as "Jack"), considered himself the "Antichrist Belarion." He engaged in the homosexual rape of a sixteen year old boy in 1942. The Pasadena police dismissed the charges and reported that the OTO was essentially "an organization dedicated to religious and philosophical speculation, with respectable members such as a Pasadena bank president, doctors, lawyers and

---

[1] At Cal Tech's Jet Propulsion Laboratory, "JPL" is also said to signify "Jack Parson Lives."

Hollywood actors."

Satanic Scientist Jack Parsons

The Masonically dominated police are far from a final word in the investigation of any lodge (in spite of often sincere efforts of well-intentioned local investigators), since one of the oaths of a Freemason states that "I will assist a Companion Royal Arch Mason when I see him engaged in any difficulty, and will espouse his cause so far as to extricate him from the same, whether he be right or wrong." [2]

Parsons' Jet Propulsion Laboratory grew out of the Harry Guggenheim-funded, Guggenheim Aeronautical Laboratory of the California Institute of Technology (GALCIT). According to Michael A. Hoffman II: GALCIT had been run by the "Hungarian-Jewish scientist Professor Theodore von Kármán, who claimed to be a direct descendant of Rabbi Judah Loew" ben Bezalel of Prague (ca. 1520-1609). "Kármán himself was a close associate of US Army General H. H. 'Hap' Arnold and an advisor to Franklin Roosevelt. Rabbi Loew in turn was the tutor of Dr. John Dee, producer of the Enochian system. Rabbi Loew is most famous, however, for the legend that he succeeded in creating artificial life, the Kabbalistic entity known as the Golem, a Gentile-destroying monster.

"Cal Tech's Jet Propulsion Laboratory was officially born on Halloween Night. A photographer captured Parsons and his colleagues in a photo now known at JPL as 'the Nativity Scene.' Each Halloween night at JPL the 'Nativity Scene' is ritually (Masonically) reenacted using mannequins as stand-ins for Parson and the others." [3]

Another JPL ritual was Parsons' invocation of the forces of Chaos before each rocket test, through a recitation of Crowley's *Hymn to Pan*. This sodomite poem was Crowley's favorite, recited at his funeral by author Louis Wilkinson. Crowley also liked to pull his orthodox Judaic sexmate Victor Neuburg's hair into two Pan-like tufts before fulfilling the poem with him. A few quotes from this poem, recited regularly at the birth of our space program, will indicate its tenor:

---

[2] Malcolm C. Duncan, *Duncan's Masonic Ritual and Monitor,* p. 230.

[3] Cf. Hoffman, "The Rocket Man" in *Secret Societies and Psychological Warfare,* pp. 200-213.

Thrill with the lissome lust of the light,
O man! My man!
Come careering out of the night
Of Pan! Io Pan!...
Devil or god, to me, to me,
My man! my man!...
Come, O come!
I am numb
With the lonely lust of devildom...
Give me the sign of the Open Eye,
And the token erect of thorny thigh...
I am borne
To death on the horn
Of the Unicorn...
And I rave; and I rape and I rip and I rend
Everlasting, world without end,
Mannikin, maiden, mænad, man....

Parsons' poetic reference to a "Mannikin" was to form an important basis for his crowning attempt at magick. His Agape Lodge was affiliated with many Hollywood writers and actors, including John Carradine, father of David Carradine, drugged-out star of "Kung Fu" and the cinematic blood-geyser "Kill Bill". The elder Carradine read one of Crowley's poems at the inauguration of Agape Lodge No. 2 in 1935. Dennis Hopper, later to splatter the screen in the "The Texas Chainsaw Massacre," acted with Parsons' Scarlet Woman, Cameron, who also knew Dean Stockwell. Filmmaker Kenneth Anger, author and producer of Hollywood Babylon, was a devoted Thelemite.

Rollo Ahmed writes: "One of his (Crowley's) pupils was a young woman we will call Magdalene. She came under his influence at any early age and has since brought havoc to all she contacts. One man committed suicide after falling under her spell. Several others were morally corrupted, and another young man who came under her influence, although he has now broken away, lives a life of seclusion in constant dread of her powers. She drove his mother away and took over the ordering of his life so that he, a man of brilliant education and talents, became unfit for anything. He woke one night after being drugged, to find that Magdalene and the man she subsequently married, were performing a death-dealing ritual with blood and candles around his bed, and they left the room congratulating themselves that he would be dead in the morning. By this time the woman was tired of him, but desired possession of his cottage and belongings. She had brought him so low that he failed to report the mysterious death and burial of an infant of hers...The woman has a nine-year-old daughter who she wishes to turn into 'The Greatest Courtesan in England.' She has a post with the BBC. She writes for certain magazines. Her tentacles stretch far."

The Homunculus

Parsons, who frequented a Communist cell, attempted to produce a "moonchild" or demonic homunculus in the womb of his Scarlet Woman, Marjorie Cameron, the "Mænad" referenced in the Hymn to Pan. This "Babalon Working" involved several abortions and confiscation of fetal tissue for government "research." The Babalon Working also included the cooperation of science fiction writer L. Ron Hubbard, who worked for US Naval Intelligence and founded the Church of Scientology, an institutionalized and bureaucratic form of Crowleyanity.

Parsons crowning achievement involved the "Mannikin" of Crowley's fevered dream. According to occult investigators James Shelby Downard and William N. Grimstad, on July 16, 1945, at the Trinity Site in New Mexico, the first atomic bomb explosion was accompanied by a huge steel "bottle" code-named "Jumbo," which weighed nearly one-half million pounds. Jumbo was twenty-five feet long and twelve feet in diameter; it had been custom-made at an eastern steel mill and expensively shipped by a sixty-four wheel trailer. Obviously, Jumbo was important to the US government. But the government has never given even a remotely reasonable explanation of Jumbo.

Downard believed that Jumbo contained what Crowley had called "the Mannikin"—an inanimate body which was inundated with nuclear energy, thus producing a real homunculus, the goal of medieval alchemy. Was fetal tissue the Mannikin or some portion of it? Given the overlapping activities of both Parsons and his government partners, the surmise is not unreasonable.

A Scientific Golem

The Golem differs from the homunculus in several respects, both represent attempts to create artificial life. The Golem is not a robot but a man. The traditional kabbalistic references to the Golem indicate that dirt or dust, and at a more cryptic, Kabbalistic level, human tissue should be present for the supposedly superior act of creation (Genesis), by which "Adam Kadmon," the body of the Divine Judaic, reverses the expulsion of Adam from Eden, demonstrating his godhood by extracting the power of the forbidden fruit from the "Tree of Life," from which the Kabbalah has derived its most famous symbol as divined by Rabbi Yitzhak Luria.

A rare glimpse of the authentic nature of Judaism can be seen in Paul Wegener's 1920 German expressionist silent film classic, "The Golem," in which Rabbi Loew consults the Kabbalah, draws a magic circle and conjures a demon to bring a Golem to life. The instructions for making a Golem are contained in the *Sefer Yetzirah*, the oldest text of the Kabbalah. The scene in the film is remarkably accurate and a far cry from "Fiddler on the Roof." (Wegener's eerie lumbering motion as the on-screen Golem was the actual model upon which the later motions of the cinematic Frankenstein monster would be based).

At Brandeis University, attempts were recently made, backed by DARPA, the U.S. "Defense Advanced Research Projects Agency," to create artificial life, beginning with attempts to "evolve" robots. The title of this military intelligence project is, "The Golem Project: Genetically Organized Lifelike Electro Mechanics". Other US agencies involved with the Golem Project are NASA, the Office of Naval Research, the Department of Defense, and the National Science Foundation. Portions of this information have been leaked and featured on National Public Radio, BBC News, and even NBC and ABC. Leaks of such information test the trance state of the public and deepen it if the public submits without protest to the disturbing signals.

The Golem has been a constant theme since cybernetics was invented in 1948, three years after the Trinity Site homunculus project with the "Mannikin," and two years after the Babalon Working with the "Maenad." During 1948—also the year of the formation of modern Israel—Jewish mathematician Norbert Wiener of the Massachusetts Institute of Technology published *Cybernetics: or Control and Communication in the Animal and the Machine.* Wiener was awarded the National Medal of Science in 1963 for his contributions in mathematics, engineering, and biological science. In 1964, shortly before he died, he published a fascinating text, *God and Golem, Inc.: A Comment on Certain Points where Cybernetics Impinges on Religion.* Echoing the passage in the

Gemara's Baba Mezia 59b, in which a Rabbi debates God
and defeats him, Wiener writes that "the conflict between
God and the Devil is a real conflict. He is actually engaged
in a conflict with his creature, in which he may very well
lose the game."

In the sub-rosa mythos of Judaism, God *is the* "Jewish
male" as personified by "Adam Kadmon" and the devil is
the force of opposition, which includes the Goyim. Hence,
Wiener's statement would also refer esoterically to the
alchemical "must Be" stage of what James Shelby
Downard called the "Revelation of the Method," in which
truths are deliberately revealed by Adam Kadmon (the
Judaic god) to the devil (the Goyim), in order to overwhelm
and defeat him, all the while knowing that real risk is
involved as a result of the exposure, and that the Judaic
Overlords "may very well lose the game." [4]

In discussing the story of the Golem allegedly made by
Loew, Wiener assesses the "danger of magic" and his
verdict is that the gamble is worth the risk. Translating
these concepts into modern cybernetic research, including
the creation of artificially intelligent machines which can
reproduce themselves, Wiener asks "why can an artificial
hand not feel?" and turns to the "mechanicohuman
system," concluding with the momentous statement that,
"The machine...is the modern counterpart of the Golem of
the Rabbi of Prague." Wiener thus stands in a line of
continuation connecting the essential work of Jack
Parsons with the current Golem Project, which is one
incarnation of the concepts advocated by Wiener.

Two researchers allegedly connected to the Golem
Project are also allegedly linked to US government
intelligence and Israel, though this writer makes no claim
of wrong-doing in this regard. One of these men was
recently posted to Cornell University; he worked from
1989-1994 for the Israeli Navy as full-time head of the
CAD/CAM Research and Development Office, after
receiving first prize for Academic Innovation in Tel Aviv in
1987. He and his alleged colleague, of Brandeis University,
an atheist who supposedly admits to being advised by a
rabbi, seemingly presented their research to joint NASA
and Department of Defense workshops in 1999 and 2000.
The title of their second presentation was "The GOLEM

---

[4] The most extensive exposition in print of Downard's theory of
the "Revelation of the Method" is found in the writings of his
protégé, Michael Hoffman II, and summarized in *Secret Societies
and Psychological Warfare.*

Project: Evolving Hardware Bodies and Brains." Both scientists posted remarks concerning their alleged project on their joint website, with the US government's DARPA insignia appearing at the bottom.

The Rodef Racket

Unmentioned is any possible role of fetal tissue in the Golem Project. According to the Talmud, the fetus may under certain circumstances be considered a *rodef* or "pursuer" of the mother, an aggressor which may be eliminated when necessary. In *Halakha*, embryos less than 40 days old are considered as mere "water." Birth control and abortion matriarch Margaret Sanger, frequently portrayed by the pro-life movement as "anti-Semitic," actually collaborated with three Judaic physicians: Hannah Stone, Bessie Moses, and Lena Levine. Stone became medical director of the Sanger clinic, and Levine helped found Planned Parenthood, the bedrock of the abortion industry. With the cultural ascendancy of such Talmudic concepts, fetal tissue experimentation was underway in the United States as early as 1939. In the 1950s, Jonas Salk used the kidney cell of fetuses to develop his polio vaccine. [5]

Probably the worst aspect of the "rodef racket" is the use of babies for live fetal experimentation, which has been conducted repeatedly by scientists, many sponsored by the National Institute of Health. Several scientists have confessed such actions with chutzpah rather than compunction. The current push by government and academia to intensify fetal tissue "research" and to engage in human cloning is one more aspect of the same Parsons' project manifested at the Trinity Site with Jumbo, the attempt to use aborted children and machines to create an alchemical Cyborg, Golem or "Terminator" through rabbinical-technological magick and usher in the final Aeon after Horus: the Aeon of Maat, proclaimed in *The Book of the Law*.

Paralleling this conspiracy is the scheme to mechanize humanity, including the dumbing-down and drugging of the populace, (resulting in beast-like dehumanization) through Paxil and Prozac, junk food, genetically-modified crops and demineralized soil, and even the induction of

---

[5] The heavily-promoted oral vaccination actually causes polio in certain people, as finally admitted by the Center for Disease Control after numerous cripples have dotted the landscape and gone in agony to their graves.

microchips and direct thought-control mechanisms. The wider Golem Project involves something at a much more expansive level, turning the Goyim as a whole into the Golem, to do the rabbinical bidding of dutifully marching off to the wars instigated by the Overlords and crushing all remaining opposition to the New World Order.

The collectivization of the White Race into one grand Golem is part of the final agenda of the Cryptocracy. As holocaust industry front-man Elie Wiesel writes in *The Golem*, "Let me tell you, we do need the Golem...in truth, the Golem had remained alive. And he is waiting to be called." [6]

The Golem is created by the real "West Nile Virus" of Egyptian/Kabbalistic patrimony, and it is not passed by mosquito but by the forces of culture, collectivizing the Goyim into the Golem through psychological alchemy. The OTO has played its role in the process. If we wish to reject the encroaching, "darker than you think" enthronement of Pan-ic, we must reject the pseudo-liberty of so-called "ethical nihilism" represented by the OTO. The lobes of the Group Mind are assessed by the Cryptocracy, and channels are triggered to respond accordingly.

The Final Aeon

The Aeon of Maat, *if* it comes to pass, will be regarded with hope or horror, depending on one's perspective. To victims of the Golem, it will be the era of Antichrist; to the multitude of Golem, it will be viewed as the prelude to a golden age. To its masters, it will be hailed as the dawn of the era of the Messiah. In such a   time, Freemasonic leaders hope to finally fulfill their Third Degree ritual by cooperating in the rebuilding of Solomon's Temple so that blood may again flow upon Jerusalem's altar, defiantly reversing and nullifying, in the Talmudic and occult mind, the blood of Christ. [7]

By calling himself "Antichrist," Parsons showed an awareness of the pivotal role of the OTO and of himself in setting the stage for these later events. As Crowley wrote to Rabbi Blau, "Let Anti-Christ arise, let Him announce to Israel its integrity. Let Him make clear the past, purged of all tribal jargon; let Him prove plainly how inevitably

[6] Elie Wiesel, *The Golem*, pp. 31 and 96.

[7] Excavations are ongoing beneath the Muslim Dome of the Rock, which must be removed to rebuild the Temple. These excavations have weakened the foundational structure of the mosque there.

event came after event." [8]

Nevertheless, the occult attempt to generate the Golem and provoke a final Aeon may produce something unpredictable, a chain reaction that could go out of control and blowback on the perpetrators. As Norbert Wiener acknowledged, risk is inherent in their game. Horus may be born, but he may be stillborn. Their glorious age may produce nothing more than a fetid corpse, a dead homunculus or D.O.A. demonic fetus as God's second greatest providential irony against a baby-killing culture since reversing the death of Christ against His executioners, bringing life to the world and driving the slave-masters of the Second Temple into dispersion and exile. In *The Island of Dr. Moreau,* the hubris and alchemy of Dr. Moreau leads to his own defeat and the defeat of his "huminal" experiments at the hands of his nightmarish creations. Author H.G. Wells knew the risks inherent in the system of Masonic sorcery, and no other work of "fiction" serves as such a potent reminder to the modern mentality, obsessed as it is with tampering with nature and man's own egotistical godhood.

Although status as the "Antichrist Belarion" and leadership role in the California OTO was known to the US government, Jack Parsons had no problem securing a top secret security clearance and finding employment with the Los Angeles Police Department, the Los Angeles Superior Court, the US Army and Navy and the National Defense Research Council. From October, 1948 until June, 1950, Parsons transferred secret documents relating to US rocket and defense technology to the Israelis. He was caught by personnel from the Propulsion and Research Development Laboratory of Hughes Aircraft, but the US Attorney declined to prosecute Parsons for treason or espionage after the intervention of Freemason J. Edgar Hoover.

"...I will assist...when I see him engaged in any difficulty, and will espouse his cause so as to be able to extricate him from the same..."

Parsons' ties to the world of science fiction did not stop with L. Ron Hubbard: his influence on Ray Bradbury and Robert Heinlein is well known in science fiction circles. Parsons himself was inspired by sci-fi writer Jack Williamson, whose novel *Darker Than You Think* dealt with werewolves conspiring against modern Christian

---

[8] "An Open Letter to Rabbi Joel Blau" in *The Revival of Magick and Other Essays,* p. 153.

civilization under the leadership of the "Child of Night," with whom Parsons obsessively identified. It is no accident that lycanthropy is a secret (along with vampirism) belonging to the upper levels of the OTO. Nor is it an accident that much of science fiction has propagandized our culture with Thelemic and Kabbalistic themes. Heinlein's books, such as *Stranger In A Strange Land* are pivotal, but the highest initiate within the genre is probably Arthur C. Clarke, who has been called a "prophet in his own future." Clarke created a mass psychological test of the hypnotic trance-state of the populace by prophesying the gradual acceptance of the rule of Satan in *Childhood's End,* a novel in which the repellent-looking Overlords come to be accepted by the people of earth as their inevitable leaders. [9]

Parsons eventually met a grisly, bloody fate, his body seared by an explosion at his "Parsonage" in Pasadena, at the age of 37. It was as if his favorite poem required one final enactment for Pan: "I rave; and I rape and I rip and I rend." His body was ripped by the explosion, "In the might of Pan."

Filmmaker Renate Druks indicated that Parsons was working on a homunculus experiment. His mother either killed herself or was murdered shortly after her son died. There are rumors that films of Parsons having sex with his own mother surfaced, post-mortem.

In his honor, in 1972 NASA named a crater after Parsons, on the dark side of the moon. John Whiteside Parsons, one may choose to believe, was honored for his work on behalf of science and humanity. One may also choose to believe that Parsons was honored for his work in ushering the planet Earth into a new Aeon—the penultimate Aeon of Horus, or, if you will, of Set or Shaitan/Satan. His work, as well as his base in Pasadena from which the Hollywood-science fiction processing of the masses was coordinated, proved of decisive value. By the time he died, in a once Christian land, it was truly dark: "darker than you think." The dark side of the moon was

---

[9] Based on a study of *Childhood's End* and Clarke's 2001 mythos (which Clarke penned in the 20th century), Hoffman wrote in April of 2001, five months before the 9/11 attacks, that the year 2001 would usher in a dramatic paradigm shift for western humanity. See "From 007 to 2001" in *Secret Societies and Psychological Warfare* (first printed in July, 2001).

the perfect homage to this man of darkness. [10]

And what of the Cult of the Beast? It has followed the usual history of secret societies; it has split into factions, spawned offshoots, suffered apparent near-extinction only to resurface in rival camps. Blood has run throughout its history, whether the blood of a menstruating Mænad, or the blood of Sharon Tate or Parsons. It has played its part in paving the way for the hoped-for Judeo-Masonic dream of rebuilding the Temple of Solomon so that the blood of animals may once again be present at the rabbinical altar.

Ground Zero: Rebuilding the Temple of Solomon

In *Born in Blood: The Lost Secrets of Freemasonry,* John J. Robinson expresses this hope: "The other problem in Israel brings us right back to Freemasonry, because it is squarely centered on the original site of the Temple of Solomon on Mount Moriah, the Temple Mount in Jerusalem, the birthplace of the Knights Templar...And for the first time in this book, we are not discussing allegories based on the temple, but the real temple, on the Temple Mount in Jerusalem....To achieve that goal on the Temple Mount would be a monumental task...A sensible plan needs to be made and then sold....What I am suggesting is that about 5 million Freemasons in the world, who do accept brotherhood with men of all faiths, in that spirit might take the lead in solving the problem of the Temple Mount by combining their religious attitudes with their veneration of the Temple of Solomon, to the benefit of the whole world."

As Rabbi Kaplan explains, "Another important consideration is the tradition that the *Bais Ha Mikdash* or Holy Temple will be rebuilt before the onset of the Messianic Age. However, there is also a tradition that Jerusalem cannot be rebuilt before the ingathering of the diaspora. This would also seem to indicate that Israel will be settled before the Messianic Age. However, it is possible that the Messiah himself will accomplish these things before he is actually recognized for what he is....It is just possible that all Jewish leaders would agree to name him their leader and confer upon him the Mosaic ordination. The chain of this ordination was broken some sixteen hundred years ago and must be renewed before the Sanhedrin...can be re-established...This is a necessary

---

[10] The classic biography of Parsons is *Sex and Rockets* by John Carter (Los Angeles: Feral House, 2000).

condition for the rebuilding of the Temple...Such a Sanhedrin would also be able to formally recognize the Messiah." [11]

Falsely billed as libertarian, some elements of the OTO have worked hoof-in-glove with the Masonic governments of the United States and England as well as Israel, allegedly engaging in espionage and receiving government protection. The plague of drug use in western countries is in no small measure due to the work of Crowley and his later successor, Timothy Leary, now carried out largely by pharmaceutical companies. An alert person cannot but notice that he is living amidst a controlled populace exhibiting so few vital signs and such limpid lethargy. The new term is "porn slump," denoting a state of fatigue and desensitization brought about by pornographic inundation, and this includes on major network television, in the form of commercials using the female anatomy to sell everything from beer to automobiles. The new drug of choice is Viagra, advertised for use with a "partner" by former Republican party presidential candidate, Senator Bob Dole, with bulging eyes and 33rd degree masonic grin.

And let us not forget the central image of the New Aeon: the Child. Crowley channeled a state in which, like a child playing with its toys or crying for milk or a diaper change, we would involve ourselves with our own will and immediate gratification. His pitch was that this new thinking would liberate us. Few would argue that our current culture is infantile, yet its liberation is highly disputable. It reflects instead, the servitude of the barnyard in George Orwell's *Animal Farm*, or, as Crowley ominously commented, "the quiet wisdom of the cattle."

The cultures of former Christendom have been re-created in the image and likeness of the Beast and "thelemized." Thelemites would say that we have benefited from this planetary initiation, holding that the aeon of self-fulfillment is an improvement over the old era with its idealization of self-sacrifice.

    If one is among the "haves and the have mores," as

[11] Aryeh Kaplan, *The Real Messiah? A Jewish Response to Missionaries,* pp. 91-93. The Israeli newspaper *Maariv* reported on Oct. 14, 2004, "After secretive preparations that lasted for over a year, the Sanhedrin – the Jewish 'Supreme Court' that consisted of 71 Torah sages – will resume its operation after 1,500 years. The modern council will consist of dozens of rabbis who are to rule on Halachaic issues and draft new Jewish rules."

President Bush jokingly called his wealthy "base" in the 2004 movie "Fahrenheit 9/11," the Aeon of Horus may look like a good deal. But if one has a child shipped back in a coffin from the Middle East, one may well see the reign of the "have mores" as not beneficial, but bestial. If the masses have become infantile children, it has not been for their liberation but rather their enslavement under a new set of child labor tycoons. Their children have a likely future as cannon fodder for an unending "War on Terror." General Tommy Franks, Commander in Chief of the United States Central Command or CENTCOM, stated, "To get information, we have to marry the devil..." [12]

Such an observation is not off-hand. It reveals the mindset of certain of our military brass, in which evil is routinely "balanced" or married to good. With our children likely to be blood sacrificed in what Tommy Franks predicts will be a "five year" occupation of Iraq, it should be clear that Set-An has not liberated us, but instead forged our chains.

The OTO blames Christianity for stifling knowledge and science. It is fair to ask: in the new Aeon, free of Biblical values, have we become more truly intelligent? Does wisdom distinguish our age? A mature person who truly feels and thinks beyond illusion can only make one assessment, although there are several gauges to prove the point. Let us take one gauge: music. Setting aside one's predilection, it is objectively undeniable that a comparison of the music of Franz Liszt and the music of rapper Snoop Dog is tantamount to comparing the work of a Ph.D. with the scribbling of a baboon; or we can speak of modern "art," some of which actually is the scribbling of a baboon.

The Wizards of Oz

We are in a universal lapse into a state of immaturity, a true indicator that we are in some sort of "era of the child." Hypnotized by computers, TVs, DVDs, CDs, palm pilots, Prozac, Paxil, and pot, the average zombie has left behind the considerations of others, as though "others" were a TV show which one could laugh at and switch off. Zombies rise in the morning, watch the morning TV shows, scan the newspapers and receive new programming, go to work, and come home to passively watch more programming. If the zombies have an original thought, it is almost invariably a selfish one. But the

---

[12] "The General Has His Say," *Parade,* August 1, 2004.

absurdity is that even the selfish thought reflects cradle-to-crypt programming from the television, that other Eye of Set.

Unless one belongs to the crowd of zombies just described, the reader will instantly (if reluctantly) recognize this description as accurate. (If the reader rejects it in anger, his hypnosis will simply deepen. Such are the risks of encountering the honest cultural mirror). The Aeon of Horus has been a major setback to world culture and human progress. In contrast to authentic human progress, "technological progress" is the advance of the Terminator, and as the Golem comes to life, it may eventually spell, through our dependence, the death of our humanity and the reign and revelation of the Overlords, the Wizards of Oz.

Such shadow-players are the true OTO Templars, the real Magicians whose wand of hypnosis exorcizes the powers of reason, and whose smoke-and-mirrors show obscures the true nature of the game. The OTO's book proclaiming a pseudo-freedom is appropriately named *Liber Oz*, (the Book of Oz). The word *"Oz"* is Hebrew for strength. The Zohar relates in 3:208a and 212a-b that all who learn magic must journey to "the mountains of darkness," the abode of the rebel angels Aza and Azael, and learn under their auspices. [13]

Aza and Azael are phonetically related to Oz. Employing Gematria, the branch of the Kabbalah devoted to numerological obsession, Oz relates to 77: 7+7=14, a number of Venus; 1+4=5, the number of the pentagram, which masonically relates to the "Five Points of Fellowship," chastely enacted in a regular Lodge, but given a fully sexual initiatory significance in higher degrees. [14]

Commenting on the relation of Oz to Venus, the pentagram, and other similar Kabbalistic equations, Kenneth Grant writes: "The unification of these concepts indicates the formula of Babalon and the Beast conjoined"—that is, the central *magica sexualis* of the OTO and the Kabbalah. [15]

---

[13] Gershom Scholem, *Kabbalah*, p. 184.

[14] Mirrored in Gerald Gardner's Third Degree of Wicca; c.f. Doreen Valiente, *The Rebirth of Witchcraft* (Custer, Washington: Phoenix Publishing, 1989), p. 56).

[15] *Aleister Crowley and the Hidden God,* p. 196.

Thus the "strength" of Oz becomes related kabbalistically in the OTO to intercourse and the "he goat," which shows the joke behind Crowley's brief text *Liber Oz*, the Book of the Goat, which is less about freedom and more about domination. This irony should be clear, reading from *Liber Oz*'s point 1, "Man has the right to live by his own law...." to its final point 5, "Man has the right to kill those who would thwart these rights." [16]

One Crowley devotee who got this "point" was Robert K. "Bobby" Beausoleil, lead guitar and sitar player for the San Francisco rock band "Magick Powerhouse of Oz." This eleven piece band, (eleven being the OTO degree for homoerotic sex magick), was assembled by avant-garde filmmaker and fellow Crowleyite Kenneth Anger, to provide the soundtrack for Anger's film project, "Lucifer Rising" which involved Led Zeppelin guitarist Jimmy Page.

"Lucifer Rising" suffered some considerable snags. Bobby Beausoleil apparently purloined much of the original 1966 footage, putting the project on hold until the 1970s, when it was resumed and shot in Egypt, England, Germany and the United States. Further problems plagued the work, however, including confiscation of the film for several years. Oz later appeared in connection with the OTO in California, following a Berkeley Police raid on Thelema Lodge, the purported Grand Lodge of the OTO from 1977-1986. After Thelema Lodge was "profaned" by the police raid, the Lodge was transformed by the OTO into Oz House.

In addition to strength, Oz relates to both brazenness and to "the Tower." Perhaps the most brazen example of the implementation of Thelemic-style dominance over a populace falsely believing in its own freedom occurred on 9/11 in 2001, in which the Twin Towers were brought down in an operation evoking the fearful specter of a hidden Magick Powerhouse—a Cryptocracy which believed in its own law, and the "right to kill" those who would intervene. These Overlords continue to operate, with *Liber Oz* being one updated version of their Kabbalistic credo, which their forebears long ago learned under Aza and Azael in the mountains of darkness.

---

[16] *The Equinox, Volume III, Number 10*, p. 144.

Skull and Bones

Another secret society has emerged as an aggressive and active arm of the Cryptocracy for the purposes of the moment: the Order of Skull and Bones.

The power of this organization has been thrust brazenly before the eyes of the Goyim: both candidates of the two major parties in the last U.S. presidential election, Bush and Kerry, were members of the Order. Skull and Bones was successfully downplayed during the 2004 campaign, reduced to a mere prankish phenomenon, a snooty Yale club consisting of capricious frat-boys and little more. But this is no laughing matter. Skulls, symbolizing necromancy and skullduggery, are at the heart of Freemasonry, whether in the "meditation room" within the lodge, or in the Kadosh ritual, in which the candidate stabs at two skulls, or in the 33rd degree, in which the candidate drinks wine out of a human skull (an act allegedly performed by George H.W. Bush). The spiritual roots of the Bonesmen are not merely masonic, but kabbalistic.

As the Zohar states, "When the desire arose in the Will of the White Head to manifest Its Glory, It arrayed, prepared, and generated from the Blinding Flash one spark...The spark congealed and one hard skull emerged, emanating to four sides. Surrounded by this pure aura, the spark was contained and absorbed. Completely absorbed, you think? No, secreted within. That is how this skull emanated to its sides. This aura is the secret of secrets of the Ancient of Days...from its side, Judgment comes into being. That is why this skull is called the Hard Skull. Inside this skull lie ninety million worlds moving with it, relying upon it."

The White Head is the bearded rulership of Adam Kadmon. The Cryptocracy maintains a necromantic Death Order rooted in associations with the Skull, the Yale Order being only one more incarnation. The Order, like all such orders, has countless people and agencies relying on it ("ninety million worlds"), and it makes key decisions while punishing deviation ("Judgment") and fomenting the Double Mind "in two colors, on this side and that." Researchers who have merely traced similarities to necromantic orders such as the Illuminati or the Nazi "Death's Head" (*Totenkopf*) have missed the crucial, conceptual kabbalistic roots behind "Tomb Raiders" like George W. Bush and John (Kohn) Kerry.

Blood on the Altar

We are approaching a critical moment in which a fateful move of the Cryptocracy will be made and in an enormous gamble, all may be won or lost, depending on whether or not we accept God-given leadership and the vision that can help us cast off the Thelemic trance.

To adapt the language of Norbert Wiener, the Cryptocracy "may very well lose the game." The Golem may turn on its master. No gambit of the Cryptocracy is foolproof; the human will remains an unpredictable natural factor, always defying the powers that be like a dandelion sprouting through a layer of seemingly impenetrable concrete. The corresponding supernatural factor is *divine gratia* or grace, an unfathomable mystery.

Unless mankind grasps this grace and reverses the alchemical-hypnotic process, struggling back to sanity, it will be harvested for one final blood offering upon the altar of dehumanization.

The human brain is inundated by 750 milliliters of blood each minute. The anatomical sacrifice demanded by the Cult of the Beast finds its locus in the skull, more specifically the brain, and, by extension, our awareness and the avenue of the soul. As *The Book of the Law* declares, "Also reason is a lie..." If we would stop invisible Golem-hands from placing a Pan-cake of brains upon the altar to "rave, rip and rend" until the very blood of the human soul covers the altar of inhumanity, then we must seek truth above all else. Contrary to the lies of the OTO, we cannot escape sacrifice. If we do not care to sacrifice time, energy, and thought in the pursuit of truth, *we* will be sacrificed. In this vein, must see the malevolent danger masked by "Judeo-Christianity," which, "in the last days" has "a form of godliness" (II Timothy 3), but is actually Crowleyanity in a rabbinical and liturgical clown costume.

The blood on the altar of God is that of Jesus Christ. It possesses all that we need for salvation. It lacks nothing.

But if we continue to reject Him by embracing a counterfeit, then it will be our blood on the altar of the OTO, sacrificed for the assurance of our damnation.

In the final analysis the OTO can do nothing without our cooperation. The OTO is only the image of what we allow to be made manifest, based on our own ignorance, myopia, sloth and fear. We must replace our processed Double Minds with the vision which is "single" (Matthew 6:22).

Glossary

Abbey of Thelema: Crowley's occult commune in Cefalù, Sicily from 1920 to 1923, called by Crowley a "Collegium ad Spiritum Sanctum" (College of the Holy Spirit). The Abbey was attacked in the press, and rumors of child sacrifice spread. Mussolini's government eventually expelled Crowley from the country.

Academia Masonica: Masonic Academy; another term for the Ordo Templi Orientis.

Adam Kadmon: Kabbalistic concept of the archetypal man, the primordial being who is simultaneously the Judaic male and the "body of God." Adam Kadmon is the androgynous and balanced, completed male Jew who manifests his own deity in this world through emanations of sefirot, which include evil in the left-hand pillar of severity or judgment—one half of which must be balanced with the opposite right-side pillar of mercy; see Tree of Life, Zohar.

Adonai, Adonay: Hebrew for "Lord," but applied to the "Holy Guardian Angel" in Thelema.

Adoptive Masonry: Groups for women and children which are related to the Masonic Lodge. Women's groups include the Order of the Eastern Star, the Daughters of Isis, and the Daughters of the Nile. Girls can join, among others, Job's Daughters and the Order of the Rainbow ("Rainbow Girls"), while boys join the Order of De Molay.

Aeon of Horus: The Age of the Child, also called the New Age and Age of Aquarius. In Thelema, this Age began in 1904 with Crowley's reception of *The Book of the Law,* replacing Christianity and its law of sacrifice with Thelema and its law of "Do what thou Will" (see Thelema).

Aeon of Isis: Supposed Matriarchal Age, when "god was a woman."

Aeon of Osiris: So-called Patriarchal Age, following the Aeon of Isis. In Thelema, Christ is equated with Osiris; hence, the Osirian Age is the Age of Christianity, based on the sacrifice of Christ. Also called the Piscean Age from Pisces the Fish (the fish was an early code symbol for

Christ during the time of persecution of Christians).

Aiwaz (also Aiwass): The preter-human intelligence which dictated the Book of the Law in 1904 to Aleister Crowley. Crowley called Aiwaz variously his "Holy Guardian Angel" and Satan.

Alchemy: The attempt to discover the "philosopher's stone," a substance capable of transmuting base metals into gold and creating the Elixir of Life. This "Hermetic" science (named after Hermes) also had a Gnostic meaning—the transmutation of (mass) consciousness. The OTO holds the semen-based Elixir to be obtained through the mixing of sexual fluids during Sex Magick, while the transformation of the masses requires ritual processes and symbolical tests and revelations.

All-Seeing Eye: See Ayin.

Anti-Mason Party: The largely forgotten major third political party in the United States which began after the Morgan assassination, operating from 1828-1837.President Filmore began his career in the Anti-Mason Party. During the height of Anti-Mason furor, John Quincy Adams demanded the suppression of Freemasonry. A United States Anti-Mason Convention met in Philadelphia on September 11, 1830.

Anti-Masonic Congress of Trent: (1896) An international congress which concluded that "the religious and philosophical doctrines reproduced and propagated by Free Masonry are the phallic doctrines of the ancient mysteries..." The Congress concluded that Freemasonry is an occult secret society in its innermost circles, which aims at the "establishment of a universal republic."

Antichrist: The final enemy of Christ's Church, described in the New Testament *Book of the Apocalypse* (or *Book of Revelation*), Chapters 13 onward, frequently as the Beast. Aleister Crowley chose the Great Beast as his title, but suggested that he was not *the* Antichrist, for he wrote to Rabbi Joel Blau of "Anti-Christ, your Messiah, who shall arise in Israel..." (*The Revival of Magick and Other Essays*, 153).

Anubis: An Egyptian deity, famous for sporting the head

of a dog; Albert Pike writes (*Morals and Dogma*, 376), that Anubis "was Sirius or the Dog-Star, the friend and counselor of Osiris, and the inventor of language, grammar, astronomy, surveying, arithmetic, music, and medical science; the first maker of laws; and who taught the worship of the Gods, and the building of Temples."

Arcanum Arcanorum: Secret of Secrets; the Grand Arcanum.

Argenteum Astrum: The AA or Silver Star. Crowley's Rosicrucian organization which emphasizes a graded initiation into the heart of the Occult Mysteries. Also called the Great White Brotherhood. The AA is said to be presided over by the "Secret Chiefs."

Ayin: An eye. The "eye in the triangle" is one of the most basic Masonic figures, exoterically the All-Seeing Eye of God, but esoterically the Eye of Set-Sothis-Shaitan (Satan); represented astronomically as Sirius and anatomically as the anus.

AA: Argenteum Astrum.

Babalon: Usually spelled in capitals, as BABALON. In Thelemic lore, Babalon is Nuit, the Egyptian sky goddess invoked as a harlot, the feminine or androgyne equivalent of Pan. The variant spelling from Babylon (see Scarlet Woman) is derived from the Enochian Calls and repeated in the *Book of the Law*. Using numerical calculations of the Kabbalah, Babalon totals 156, the number for Zion as well as the number of pyramids on each Enochian tablet. Part of Thelemic sex magick involves an attempt to unite Chaos and Babalon through intercourse, in imitation of the completion of the perfected androgynous divinity, Adam Kadmon.

Baphomet: (Goat of Mendes; Goat of the Sabbath): Capricornus, the Devil: the "god of lust," whose horns fit within the two uppermost points of the inverted pentagram of the Black Magician. The OTO teaches that "SATAN...is "The Devil" of the Book of Thoth (Tarot cards), and His emblem is BAPHOMET..." Also see: Eliphas Levi.

Bataille, Dr. Henri: Alias of Dr. Carl Hackse, an author who wrote extensively of the Palladium. Dr. Hackse later mysteriously denounced his own writings.

Beast: Derived from the New Testament *Book of the Apocalypse* (or *Book of Revelation*), Chapter 13. Crowley's title for himself: TO MEGA QHRION, The Great Wild Beast, which totals 666 in Greek.

Blue Lodge: The basic unit of a Grand Lodge; the local Lodge. Also called the Regular Lodge or Craft Lodge. Many Blue Lodges have blue ceilings (some with stars), signifying the open sky under which ancient Masons are said to have met. To some High Degree Masons, astrological and solar-phallic meaning is read into this symbol.

Ceremonial Magic (High Magic, Transcendental Magic): Sorcery which typically contains both ritual invocation and evocation of spirits. Renamed "Magick" by Crowley, to distinguish it from sleight-of-hand stagecraft.

Chaos: 1. In Thelemic doctrine, the totality of the units of existence. 2. The father principle, as "Babalon" is the mother.

Co-Masonry: Irregular Freemasonry which admits women as well as men (mixed Lodges). Annie Besant, 33°, the successor of Madame Blavatsky as President of the Theosophical Society, founded the English Branch of Co-Masonry in 1902. She was Vice-President Grand Master of the Supreme Council, and Deputy for Great Britain and its Dependencies.

Compass: One of the Great Lights in Freemasonry, and part of the symbol on every regular Lodge. Lower Masons are taught that the compass symbolizes the circumscribing of our actions to keep them "within bounds" (moral meaning). 32nd Degree Masons learn that the compass has a phallic meaning too, symbolizing the "procreative and generative agents...the Hermetic Symbol of the Creative Deity." (Albert Pike, *Morals and Dogma*, 851).

Concealed Child: 1. New Aeon before its birth in 1904. (See Aeon of Horus). 2. Harpocrates, the "self unmanifest."

Conjuration: Evocation; calling forth a spirit to do one's bidding. Part of Magick. Also, calling forth a state of mass consciousness.

Craft, The: 1. Freemasonry, so-called because the organization developed from the medieval craft of masonry. 2. Wicca, which in its Gardnerian form, utilizes the structure of Freemasonry for initiation, since Wicca was largely developed by Freemasons Gerald Gardner and Aleister Crowley.

Crowned and Conquering Child: 1. the New Aeon after its birth in 1904 (Aeon of Horus). 2. The self manifest, also called Horus and Ra-Hoor-Khuit.

Daughters of the Nile: Exclusive Adoptive Masonic group open only to the wives of Shriners, by invitation only.

De Molay, Jacques: Grand Master of the Knights Templar. The Masonic Order of De Molay for boys is named for him. De Molay was burned at the stake. High Grade Freemasonry reveals that Hiram Abiff represents De Molay, and the vengeance against his assassins is to be directed against "thrones and altars," or resistant national governments and the Church. Initiation into this meaning is given slowly (see, for example, the 30th Degree ritual in the Scottish Rite, and the Sixth Degree ritual in the OTO).

Enneagram, Enneagon: Nine-sided kabbalistic figure in occultism discussed at length in Golden Dawn instructions. The Enneagram has since spread (erroneously) as a form of "personality typing."

Enochian Calls: These "Nineteen Calls" were magical invocations of spirit beings, obtained by the Elizabethan medium Edward Kelly. They became the basis of the "Angelic Secret Language" known as *Enochian*, formulated by Queen Elizabeth I's astrologer, John Dee, an accomplished mathematician. The Calls were undertaken by Aleister Crowley and Victor Neuburg in 1909 in the Algerian desert, where they summoned entities and experienced demonic possession (during one such rite Crowley cried out, "I am Satan!"). Generally, rites based on the Enochian Calls are hedged by grave warnings in the Golden Dawn and the OTO.

Evocation: In occultism, the "calling forth" of a spirit in an attempt to control it, or, at a deeper level, calling forth a specific and determined state of consciousness in the masses.

Exoteric: The aspect of a Gnostic religion, secret society, or occult Order shared with the average lower member or even the general public.

Fama Fraternitatis: Work written in 1614 proclaiming the existence of the occult order of Rosicrucians. Attributed to Lutheran clergyman Johann Valentin Andrea (1586-1654).

Fez: Red hat worn by the Shriners. The legendary figure Christian Rosenkreutz, alleged founder of the Rosicrucians, is said to have deepened his knowledge of Occultism in Fez, Morocco.

Freemasonry: A vast international organization utilizing the symbols of the trade of masonry as an alphabet of gradual initiation for members sworn to secrecy. Members are ritually pledged in the Royal Arch Degree to the "good" of "the Jewish nation in particular" and, in the Kadosh Degree to attack the Catholic Church and sovereign governments. Members are also pledged to favoritism and protection for other Freemasons, including concealment of murder and treason. Death symbols and images such as skulls and an obsession with veiled sexual imagery, gradually unfolded to initiates, are standard aspects of Freemasonic ritual and metaphor. Officially dated from 1717, according to Michael A. Hoffman II, Freemasonry was actually germinated by Queen Elizabeth I's court occultist, the English mathematician and necromancer John Dee (1527-1609), under the direction of the leading Kabbalist of the age, Rabbi Judah Loew of Prague. Freemasonry's large membership includes many members of government, police, and the judiciary, forming what Johann Wolfgang von Goethe (1749-1832) called "a state within a state."

Gardner, Gerald Brosseau: (1884-1964). With the help of Aleister Crowley, Gardner founded modern Wicca. Gardnerian Wicca differs in some ways from Traditional Witchcraft, and is modeled on the Lodge (Gardner was a Freemason) and the OTO.

Gnosis: The Greek word for knowledge, used by adepts to refer to secret knowledge or insight. The Gnostics were a branch of Judaic Kabbalists masquerading as Christians, viewed as a deceptive threat and a subject of great concern by early Church fathers such as Irenaeus of Lyons (A. D. 120-202).

Gnostic Mass: The central and public ritual of the ecclesiastical arm of the OTO, the "Gnostic Catholic Church." Composed by Aleister Crowley in 1920.

Gnostic Catholic Church: The "Ecclesiastica Gnostica Catholica" (EGC), the worldwide ecclesiastical wing of the OTO.

Gnosticism: Heavily influenced by rabbis, historically Gnosticism involved a belief that the world was made by a limited creator called the Demiurge (*Keter* in the Kabbalah), a being who must be transcended by finding the god beyond this being (Lucifer the Light Bearer, or in the Kabbalah, *Ain Soph Aur*, the Light of Limitless Nothingness). Crowley writes in *The Vision and the Voice* (120) of the "*demiurgus,* Microprosopus, the Black Reflected Countenance, the Creator."

Golden Dawn, Hermetic Order of: Influential occult society of the British intellectual avant-garde, named after Lucifer the Light-Bearer--"bringer and herald of the Dawn." Founded in 1865 by eminent Freemasons claiming Rosicrucian initiation. Prominent members of the Golden Dawn included distinguished figures in English literature such as William Butler Yeats, Algernon Blackwood, Arthur Machen and Florence Farr; as well as S.L. MacGregor Mathers, A.E. Waite and Aleister Crowley. Apologists for the Golden Dawn claim Crowley was expelled due to his work with black magic. While it is true that some of the Luciferians in the Golden Dawn resented Crowley's rampant drug use and homosexuality --fearing it would bring unwelcome public scrutiny and notoriety-- recent scholarship has shown that Crowley was purged as the result of a "bitter power struggle." Publication of Golden Dawn materials by Israel Regardie helped spur the occult revival of the 20th century.

Grand or Great Arcanum: The "Great Secret" of the Magician which signifies Gnostic insight and occult attainment. The Great Work is the personal discovery of the Arcanum.

Grand Lodge: The administrative authority in Freemasonry in its territory ("jurisdiction"). The first official Grand Lodge was formed in 1717 in London's "Apple Tree" and "Devil's Tree" Taverns.

Great White Brotherhood: Term for the "Secret Chiefs," or, in the language of Arthur C. Clarke, "the Overlords." Demonic entities in direct contact and administrative relationship awith humans. This concept has been foreshadowed many times in legend; cf. for example the enigma of "Prester John."

Great Work: The goal of Magick. In essence, becoming a god and mastering or "perfecting" the universe through Gnosis. The Great Work involves the belief that the order of creation is inadequate and needs the superior insight of the magician to improve on God's own handiwork. Modern scientism can be viewed as a branch of the Great Work; a literary evocation of this phenomenon is contained in *The Island of Dr. Moreau* by H. G. Wells (1866-1946)..

Hadit: An Egyptian god, symbolizing a paradoxically small yet omnipresent point (or point of view) in Thelemic theology, as well as motion. The interplay of Hadit (motion) and Nuit (matter) produce the universe. See Hera-Ra-Ha.

Hall, Manly Palmer: (1901-1990). 33rd Degree Freemason and founder of the Philosophical Research Society, in 1934 His works propagandize on behalf of the occult and are highly recommended by Freemasons, although riddled with historical errors and fantastic claims of masonic provenance.

Harpocrates: An Egyptian god, symbolizing in Thelemic theology the higher self, the god of silence containing everything while remaining unmanifested. Also called the Concealed Child and the "Holy Guardian Angel."

Hell: In Thelemic doctrine, Hell is positive, the "Secret Centre of the Self" (Aleister Crowley, *The Vision and the Voice*, 81).

Hermetic: Pertaining to Alchemy in a symbolical sense, as the transmutation of the "base metal" of normal consciousness into the "gold" of Gnostic insight for the elite, and hypnotic servitude for the masses. The term is derived from Hermes Trismegistus ("thrice-greatest Hermes"), the Greek god also known as Thoth of the Egyptians, and revered by occultists as the teacher of wisdom.

Heru-Ra-Ha: An Egyptian deity, the offspring of Nuit and Hadit, which combines in Thelemic theology the twin ideas of Ra-Hoor-Khuit and Hoor-paar-kraat.

Hexagram: Six-sided figure with intersecting lines. Derived from kabbalistic occultism, Hexagram rituals are common in Magick, symbolizing the androgynous union of opposites in the completed and divinized male, Adam Kadmon. Widely and erroneously known as the "Star of David," the hexagram had nothing to do with King David historically. The Square and Compass of Freemasonry is an incomplete hexagram, symbolizing that the Freemason is an incomplete Jew, and therefore a servant of those who possess the completed hexagram, the kabbalistic-rabbinic masters. Freemasons are pledged ritually to their service.

Hidden Masters: A term for the Secret Chiefs.

High Magic: See Ceremonial Magic.

High Grade, High Degree: Freemasonry which extends beyond the Third Degree of the ordinary Grand Lodge system. The High Degrees claim to unfold deeper insight into the first Three Degrees but do not replace them. A Master Mason (Third Degree), is exoterically fully initiated, but can achieve a deepening esoteric initiation through insight into his own initiation and its subtler meaning, through Gnosis. High Degrees assist this process and are obtained through the Ordo Templi Orientis (OTO).

Holy Ari: Rabbi Isaac Luria (1534-1572),, also "Rabbi Yitzhak ben Shlomo Luria," regarded as the greatest of all Kabbalists. Ari is an acronym for *Ha Eloki Rabbeinu Yitzhak*, "the godly Rabbi Yitzhak." Rabbi Luria is most famous for his articulation of the symbol called the Tree of Life.

Holy Guardian Angel: Aleister Crowley considered his Holy Guardian Angel variously as both Aiwaz and Satan. It is also synonymous in OTO lore with Harpocrates, the unmanifest or Silent Self, personified in a spirit whose "knowledge and conversation" is sought. The basis of seeking the "Holy Guardian Angel" in Thelema is found in a possibly spurious "Qabalah text" employed by Aleister Crowley called *The Sacred Magic of Abra-Melin the Mage,* allegedly written by a Judaic adept.

Horus: In Egyptian theology, the infant son of Isis, "the Crowned and Conquering Child."

Illuminati: Founded in Bavaria on May 1, 1776 by an adept using the symbolic pseudonym "Adam Weishaupt," the Illuminati copied Jesuit discipline and mobilized the engine of Freemasonry for occult dictatorship. The OTO professes to continue the initiation of the Illuminati.

Illuminism: Broadly, the pursuit of an inner spiritual light through a Gnostic approach. In a narrower sense, the dogma of the Bavarian Illuminati Initiated illuminists seek enlightenment from Lucifer, the Light Bearer and herald of the Golden Dawn.

Irregular Mason: A Freemason whose lodge is not officially sanctioned by a Grand Lodge. Many irregular lodges interact with Grand Lodges, however, in spite of denials. The mask of "irregularity" gives convenient grounds for "plausible denial" and serves to protect the conservative image of regular Freemasonry.

Isis. The supreme goddess of ancient Egypt who commands magic and the "words of power" (twilight language), and whose emblematic star is Sothis (Sirius). In voodoo and other superstitious sects with a Catholic veneer, Isis is venerated disguised as the Blessed Virgin Mary. In Protestant England Isis was revered by the secret societies in the person of Queen Elizabeth I. In 1921, in Cefalu, Sicily, Aleister Crowley performed an "invocation to the Holy Spirit" in the form of the solemn litany to Isis:
Cf. http://archives.bapho.net/C/C0000199/C0000199.html

Jah-Bul-On: The syncretic "Grand Omnific Word" given to Masons "exalted" to the Seventh or Royal Arch Degree.

Taught as the name of God, it is the symbolic compound of Jehovah, Baal, and Osiris. The word is given in the Fourth Degree in the OTO.

Job's Daughters: A Masonic Order for girls; a type of juvenile Freemasonry.

Kabbalah: The sacred books of black magic of orthodox Judaism which form a large part of the basis of the western secret societies, from Rosicrucianism to Freemasonry and the OTO. Kabbalism is itself derived from the sorcery of ancient Babylon and Babylon's progenitor, Pharaonic Egypt.

Kadosh, Knight: 30th Degree in Scottish Rite Freemasonry. A series of skulls are stabbed in the revolutionary ritual of this rite. Kadosh in Hebrew means "holy" or "consecrated." The true Kadosh is the completed Kabbalistic being, Adam Kadmon. Spelled Kadosch in the Sixth Degree of the OTO.

Kelipah: "husk" or "shell;" plural kelipot. Also qliphoth. In the Kabbalah, the impure kelipot, or *shalosh kelipot temeiot*, are the domain of evil and the demonic realm from which the souls of all Gentiles (*Goyim*) emanate, as taught in the Chabad- Lubavitcher holy book, *Tanya,* chapter 2, as well as in *Etz Chayyim*, Portal 49, chapter 3. This higher kabbalistic secret is typically withheld from goyim seeking initiation, until they are sufficiently conditioned to embrace their Overlords.

Knife and Fork Mason: The typical Freemason who attends the lodge for largely social and business reasons. Such members are usually ignorant of any deeper meaning in Freemasonry beyond its superficial moral and ecumenical instruction. These masons serve the important purpose of preserving a conservative and respectable image for the institution.

Kundalini: In Hinduism, the "Serpent Power" lying at the base of the spine. Aroused, it either travels downward as sexual desire, or up the spine through the chakras to lead to spiritual insight, according to occult theory. In Judaism a parallel concept is taught as part of the "Esoteric Wisdom." Cf. Adin Steinsaltz, *Opening the Tanya: Discovering the Moral and Mystical Teachings of a Classic*

Work of Kabbalah.

Landmarks: Foundational and indispensable matters of Masonic law; sometimes called the "Unwritten Law" of Masonry as opposed to the Constitutions or "Written Law" of Masonry. The Landmarks date to the early 18th century.

Lemmi, Adriano: (1822-1906). Important Italian Freemasonic leader, accused of being a leader (together with Albert Pike) of a Satanic inner circle, the Palladium.

Level: One of the tools of the Fellow Craft Mason (2nd Degree), explained as a reminder that we are traveling on the "level of time to that undiscovered country from whose bourne no traveler has returned." (cf. Captain William Morgan, *Freemasonry Exposed*, 56) "Are you on the level?" is an old coded question asked by a Mason to determine if another person is also a Mason. It is so ubiquitous it has entered American culture as a byword for a test of one's integrity.

Levi, Eliphas (or Éliphas Lévi Zahed): (1810-1875). Born Alphonse Louis Constant. French occultist notorious for his "Sigil of Baphomet" illustration which was reproduced in rock-and-roll music and youth culture throughout the 1960s and 1970s. His most important works are *The Dogma and Ritual of High Magic* and *Transcendental Magic*. Albert Pike borrowed extensively from Levi's writings for *Morals and Dogma*. Levi was also an important source for Theosophist Helena Blavatsky and Aleister Crowley. The latter claimed to be the reincarnation of Levi. A columnist for the San Francisco-based *Gnosis Magazine* alleges that Levi was "an always faithful Catholic." Most informed Catholics would say otherwise.

Light: In Freemasonry the continual goal of one's quest. In the Higher Grades, one learns that this inner illumination comes from Lucifer. (Albert Pike, *Morals and Dogma*, 321).

Lodge: Meeting place or unit of Freemasonry.

Luther, Martin: (1483-1546). German monk and father of the Lutheran religion. According to Crowley's kabbalistic perspective of Thelema, Luther's "magical act of cohabitation with a nun" helped prepare the way for the Aeon of Horus (Aleister Crowley, *The Vision and the Voice*, 196). Also see: Fama Fraternitatis.

Magick: Ceremonial magic, generally described by Crowley as, "the science and art of causing change to occur in conformity with will." More narrowly, sorcery or the conjuration of spirits. Of this narrower meaning, Jean Bodin gave the following definition: "A sorcerer is one who by commerce with the Devil has a full intention of attaining his own ends."

Magnum Opus: The Great Work.

Magus: A master of Magick. In the AA, the grade of Magus (9°=2°), is next to the highest degree. The Magus utters a Word which transforms the planet; Crowley's word was Thelema, allegedly initiating the world into the Aeon of Horus.

Maitreya: "World Teacher." An incarnation of Buddha and a title appropriated by Aleister Crowley and certain New Age leaders.

Master Mason: A Mason of the Third Degree. Higher Degrees only gradually unfold the Gnostic teachings latent by symbolism in this highly dramatic degree. In this sense the Grand Lodge is correct in saying Higher Degrees add nothing, but conversely, without the Higher Degrees most Masons never understand the meaning of the lower grades except in hoodwinked terms of trite moral lessons.

Matrona: In the Kabbalah, the Shekhinah, the feminine aspect of deity invoked during sex magick. This term is occasionally encountered in occultism rather than its Hebrew equivalent.

Memphis Rite: A system of High Degree Freemasonry which contained 97 degrees, now imparted by the OTO.

Mizraim Rite: A system of High Degree Freemasonry which contained 90 degrees, now imparted by the OTO.

Morality: In occultism, a code of behavior determined by oaths and related to keeping to one's defined purpose and absorbing all activities within that purpose.

Morals and Dogma: Key textbook of the occult mysteries traditionally distributed to High Degree Scottish Rite Masons. Written by Grand Commander Albert Pike for the Supreme Council of the Thirty-Third Degree. The book progressively reveals, among many other secrets: 1). that the Kabbalah is the inner essence of Freemasonry, and 2). this fact is deliberately hidden from lower degree Masons.

Morgan, William: Royal Arch Mason who published the rituals of Freemasonry in 1826, earning his kidnapping and murder by fellow Masons who doubled as county and state officials in New York, a murder which rocked the young Republic, causing numerous masonic lodges in the northeast to be closed and leading to the creation of the Anti-Mason Party in the U.S.

Mormon: A member of the religion taught by Master Mason Joseph Smith (1805-1844). Mormon temple rituals and symbols contain many aspects similar or identical to the rituals and symbols of Freemasonry. Mormons claim that Joseph Smith restored the original Freemasonry. Masons considered Joseph Smith to have violated his Masonic oaths and as a consequence, murdered him. Evidence of Smith's involvement with the occult is offered in a book by D. Michael Quinn, Professor of History at Brigham Young University, *Early Mormonism and the Magic World View*.

Nuit: The Egyptian sky goddess, symbolizing infinite space (matter's condition or "form") in Thelemic theology. Time is also included in Nuit as a dimension of space. The interplay of Nuit (matter) and Hadit (motion) produce the universe as personified by Isis and Osiris.

Operative Mason: A person whose trade is building with stones and bricks, as opposed to speculative (occult) "Free"-masonry. Originally the stonemasonry trade was a Medieval Catholic guild.

Order of the Eastern Star: Largest women's group of Adoptive Masonry. Created by Freemason Rob Morris in 1850, the Order is supposedly Christian, but their pentagram is well-known by initiated Masons to have another meaning.

Ordo Templi Orientis (OTO) The Order of Oriental Templars. A modern system of High Degree Freemasonry which aims to distill the occult and political aspects of Freemasonry at the most advanced level of initiation, thus incorporating and including all other forms of Freemasonry. The OTO was established around the turn of the Twentieth Century by consolidating the Hermetic Brotherhood of Light and the Masonic Rites of Memphis and Mizraim.

Palladium: Allegedly a super-rite of the cult of Lucifer practiced within the innermost circles of High Degree Freemasonry. A new and reformed Palladium Rite was allegedly created by Albert Pike.

Pan: Mythological figure equated in the occult with Baphomet and (when the initiate is deemed ready), the Devil—as well as the deepest state of occult trance.

Pantacle (Pentacle): The flat, waxen disk upon which the magician works, typically engraved and consecrated. The popular enneagram is a traditional kabbalistic inscription on the pantacle in magick.

Papus: Encausse, Gérard (1865-1916). Head of the occult/Gnostic Martinist Order and the French OTO. Dr. Encausse published his occult writings under the pseudonym Papus.

Parrot Mason: A Mason who thoughtlessly memorizes and repeats his lessons without inquiring further for the Light of Freemasonry.

Pass-Grip: Handshake by which Masons recognize each other. These differ according to the degree of the member, and normally involve a pressing of the thumb between certain knuckles during the handshake.

Pentagram: Five-sided star-like figure, typically drawn with intersecting lines, used in Masonry and the occult as well as being a symbol of police and military forces worldwide, representing the blazing star Albert Pike identified as Sirius.

Pike, Albert: (1809-1891) Sovereign Grand Commander of the Scottish Rite of Freemasonry. Author of *Morals and*

Dogma. Early member of the Theosophical Society. Confederate General accused of directing Indian troops in atrocities against Union soldiers at the Battle of Pea Ridge during the War Between the States.

Prince Hall Freemasonry: Irregular Lodge of Freemasonry for Black men, dating to the acceptance of fourteen Blacks (including Prince Hall) into a Military Lodge of the British army at Boston on March 6, 1775. Under much intense exposure and pressure, a few regular Lodges have begun to admit Blacks today. One of the most famous of the Prince Hall Freemasons is Jesse Jackson (Harmony Lodge No. 88, Chicago, Illinois)

Qabalah: The version of the esoteric, "wonder-working" Judaic scriptures associated with the gentile-based secret societies such as the Hermetic Order of the Golden Dawn and the OTO. This "Qabalah" usually relies upon the same rabbinic texts which comprise Judaism's "Kabbalah," but are accompanied by a corpus of commentary and speculation with "New Age" and "Aquarian" themes, by such luminaries of the western secret societies as Aleister Crowley, Samuel Liddell MacGregor Mathers, "Eliphas Levi" (Alphonse Louis Constant), Frater Achad (Charles Stansfield Jones) and "Dion Fortune" (Violet Mary Firth). The alternate spelling has recently lost ground to "Kabbalah", which appears more rabbinic and therefore supposedly more authentic, and certain 19th and 20th century texts published originally with "Qabalah" in the title are being reissued with the allegedly more sophisticated "Kabbalah" rendering.

Ra-Hoor-Khuit: An Egyptian god, symbolizing in thelemic theology a unity which includes and heads all things. A conjunction of Nuit and Hadit. Also, the twin or active form of Harpocrates—the manifest self as opposed to the unmanifest.

Regardie, Israel: (1907-1985) Secretary to Aleister Crowley; member of the Golden Dawn.

Regular Mason: A Freemason under the jurisdiction of a Grand Lodge.

Rosicrucian: A follower of an occult practice involving an esoteric interpretation of the central sexual symbol of the

Rose and the Cross, or Rosy Cross. The organization was instrumental in processing western humanity away from Christianity and into the occult.

Royal Arch: The Seventh Degree in the York Rite of Freemasonry, in which Masons are "exalted" and receive the Grand Omnific Word (Jah-Bul-On) and pledge themselves "for the good of Masonry in general, and the Jewish nation in particular." Viewed as a culmination of the ordinary Three Degrees, Royal Arch workings are conducted in a Chapter under the control of a Grand Chapter rather than a Grand Lodge. In the OTO, this degree is the Fourth rather than the Seventh.

Sacrament: In the Roman Catholic Church, a Sacrament is an outward sign instituted by Christ to give grace. Seven Sacraments are enumerated: Baptism, Confirmation, the Holy Eucharist, Penance, Extreme Unction, Holy Orders, and Matrimony. The Gnostic Catholic Church also administers its own version of sacraments, and the sex magick of the IX° in the OTO is valued in part for producing a "eucharist" of fluids which is consumed by the participants.

Saint-Martin: (1743-1803). Marquis Louis Claude de Saint-Martin, known as the "unknown Philosopher;" Saint-Martin reformed the occult Martinist Order in 1775. The Martinist Order had been founded earlier in 1754 by Martines de Pasqually (d. 1774). Arthur Edward Waite (*New Encyclopaedia of Freemasonry*, II, 394), writes that "Saint-Martin's first book was a Bible—or Talmud at least—for French High Grade Masons on the eve of the Revolution." The Martinists were later headed by Dr. Gérard Encausse ("Papus"), also the French leader of the OTO.

Satan: Literally, the "adversary." Thelemites invoke and honor Satan but paradoxically reject as erroneous the label "Satanist."

Scarlet Woman: Derived from the New Testament *Book of the Apocalypse (Book of Revelation)*, Chapter 17, where she is also called *Babylon*, the Great Whore.

Scottish Rite (Southern Jurisdiction): The most powerful branch of Freemasonry in the world. Developed in France (not Scotland), this Rite was rewritten and amplified by Albert Pike, who established the first Thirty-Third Degree Supreme Council of the Ancient and Accepted Scottish Rite of Freemasonry in Charleston, South Carolina. The name "Scottish" is symbolic. According to William N. Grimstad in his "Sirius Rising" lectures, it is a tribute to powers Freemasons associate with Scotland.

Secret Chiefs: Allegedly the leaders behind the *Argenteum Astrum*—responsible for ushering humanity into various initiatory "aeons," the current phase being the Aeon of Horus. "The Order of the Silver Star is thus the Order of the Eye of Set, 'the Sun behind the Sun'...The Silver Star is Sirius." (Kenneth Grant, *Aleister Crowley and the Hidden God*). Among the earliest physical references to these beings is found in connection with the terrestrial lore surrounding the "silver star" Sirius. In myth they are personified as the "Nommos" and as "Oannes." The Nommos are also called "The Monitors, The Instructors" and "The Repulsive or Repellent Ones". In *Childhood's End*, Arthur C. Clarke referred to them as the "Overlords."

Sefer HaGilgulim: "The Book of Reincarnation." This key kabbalistic text is based on the teachings of Rabbi Isaac Luria and edited by Rabbi Meir Popperos. Reincarnation or *gilgul* is an important teaching in Hasidic and Sephardic Judaism.

Serpent: In the Kabbalah, the serpent has an important role. The "Serpent of Wisdom" binds together the twenty-two paths of the Tree of Life. Explaining the 25th Degree of Freemasonry—Knight of the Brazen Serpent—Albert Pike writes that the "Cosmogeny [sic] of the Hebrews and that of the Gnostics designated this reptile as the author of the fate of souls." (*Morals and Dogma*, 492)

Sex Magick: A jealously guarded secret of the Kabbalah. In the OTO, full sex magick is taught in the Ninth Degree.

Shriners (or Mystic Shrine): The "Ancient Arabic Order, Nobles of the Mystic Shrine" began in 1872. Open only to Masons who have achieved the degrees of either the Scottish or York Rite, the Shriners have a reputation for establishing crippled children's hospitals, circuses and for whimsical parades, giving the occult an appearance of benevolence and innocence. On the lesser known side, the Shriner oath commits the Shriner to receive the Masonic penalty for transgressions by "having my eyeballs pierced to the center." The "shrine" reference is to the legendary repository in Damascus, Syria said to contain John the Baptist's severed head. While Shriners burlesque "Arab mysteries," the veneration they pay is actually to Pharaonic Egypt, not orthodox Islam, with its enmity toward idolatry, usury, political corruption and other masonic staples.

Sorcery: The practice of invocation and evocation through visualization and ritual. Crowley's system was called Magick. In a deeper sense, Masonic sorcery pertains to the control and alchemical processing of the consciousness of the masses, the Group Mind.

Speculative Mason: An occult mason as opposed to a bricklayer; someone initiated through a symbolic reference to the tools of masonry.

Square: One of the "Great Lights" in Freemasonry, and part of the symbol on every regular Lodge. Lower Masons are taught that the square symbolizes squaring our actions (moral meaning). 32nd Degree Masons learn that the square has a vulvar meaning, symbolizing the "productive Earth or Universe," its "material, sensual, and baser portion." (Albert Pike, *Morals and Dogma*, 851).

Talisman: Kabbalistic object engraved with symbolic markings and traditionally consecrated after conjuring the spirits of darkness. Instructions for talismans in Judaism are contained in the Sefer Rezial Hemelach, or *Book of the Angel Rezial*. One famous religious founder to wear a talisman (a Jupiter talisman) was Joseph Smith (see Mormon).

Templar, Knights: The Knights Templar Order was founded in 1118 by Hugh de Payens. Originally blessed by the Catholic Church, it was later suppressed when the worship of Baphomet was discovered in its ranks. The top degree of the mock-Christian York Rite of Freemasons is Knight Templar, while the OTO signifies the Order of the Oriental Templars.

Temple: In masonic ritual, the building of the Temple of

Solomon in Jerusalem is interrupted and left to be finished later. The Temple has many meanings, including Gnostic (building a spiritual temple of occult insight). Masons are pledged as the helpers of Judaism through the symbolism of the Third Degree ritual, reinforced more explicitly in the Royal Arch degree; therefore one fundamental Masonic aim is the reconstruction of the Temple of Solomon in Jerusalem. The Masonic Temple itself is in the form of a large cube, symbolic of the universe. Like other magickal work the sex magick of the OTO also occurs within the "templo" or temple.

Thelema: From the Greek, meaning free will. Derived from the literary Abbey of Thélème of Francois Rabelais' *Gargantua* (1534), a novel consisting of densely philosophical syncretism and stinging satire of the Church. Rabelais presents the Abbey of Thélème as a kind of freedom-soaked paradise. But Catholic philosopher Thomas Molnar describes it as a snare, a "counter-church" which, beneath its hedonistic facade, has rules more rigid than that of the Church. The motto of Thélème is *Fais ce que voudras*--"Do what you will." Molnar translates it in the argot of the hippies: "Do your own thing." Thelema was said by Aleister Crowley to signify both the matrix through which the OTO's system of magick flows, magnifies and gains momentum, and the religion wherein one finds and follows one's True Will under Horus.

Theurgy: The conjuration or evocation of spirits through ritual as the "practical" aspect of Kabbalah.

Third Degree: 1. The top "Master Mason" degree in a regular Blue Lodge. Masons at this level are "raised" to the degree through a ceremonial reenactment of the assassination and resurrection of Hiram Abiff, architect of Solomon's Temple, whose part the candidate unexpectedly plays blindfolded—a dramatic surprise. 2. Brutal interrogation.

Thirty-Third Degree: An honorary degree, the 33° is the highest degree in Scottish Rite Freemasonry. Most Freemasons erroneously believe that no system of degrees exists above this one; but the OTO supplies the higher degrees of "Egyptian" Masonry: Memphis and Mizraim.

Tiara, Papal: Triple crown traditionally worn by the Pope on solemn occasions, signifying his threefold dignity as bishop of Rome, pastor of the Universal Church (Vicar of Christ), and, politically, as a head of state (Rome). A mock papal tiara on a skull is stabbed in the Knight Kadosh Degree (30th in the Scottish Rite). A parallel ritual occurs in the Sixth Degree of the OTO.

Tree of Life: *Etz Chayyim*. In the Bible, the tree which would have conferred eternal life, but which God guarded by angels and a flaming sword after man sinned (Genesis 3:23-24). In the Kabbalah, the Tree of Life (developed by Isaac Luria [1534-1572]), is a symbol of both the cosmos and the soul, set in a pattern of ten emanations from the divine Adam Kadmon, called *sefirot* (or *sephiroth*), plural form of *sefirah*. These emanations are placed in this schema within two pillars, Severity and Mercy, signifying the Double Mind. The Middle Pillar is the secret of equilibrium and control for the kabbalistic adept. At an advanced level, the rabbinic teaching indicates that the initiate must follow the "descent" of Abraham taught in the Zohar and therefore must explore the demonic contained in the Nightside or negative side of the Tree. *Etz Chayyim* is also the title of an important works of the Kabbalah, based mostly on the teachings of Luria. The Tree of Life is completely central to the magick of the western secret societies.

Typhon: In Egyptian mythology, the slayer of Osiris.

Vaughan, Diana: Alleged Grand Mistress of "the Palladium", who, after a conversion to the Catholic Church, wrote memoirs exposing the sex magick and occultism of the Palladium. Vaughan was later denounced as a fraudulent literary invention, although Dr. Israel Regardie testifies to having seen a Palladium charter which was signed by her and Leo Taxil, who first wrote of the Palladium.

Wicca: A modern, popularized version of OTO-style magick. Originally replete with Freemasonic initiation rituals (slightly varied by instrument, wording or absence of clothing), Wicca is in one sense a revival of Witchcraft and in another sense a new creation, originated by Freemasons Gerald Gardner and Aleister Crowley.

York Rite: Also called American Rite. A system of

Freemasonry which culminates in a Thirteenth Degree with the title Knight Templar. The York Rite carries the Royal Arch Degree and mocks rituals of Christianity while advertising itself as a Christian Rite.

Zohar: "Brilliance" or "Splendor." One of the fundamental scriptures of the Kabbalah, allegedly compiled by Rabbi Shim'on bar Yochai (Simon ben Yohai), in the second century, but dated by some scholars (especially Gershom Scholem) to 1280-86, with authorship attributed to Rabbi Moses de León, in Spain. Rabbi ben Yohai is most notorious for his statement in the Talmud (Soferim 15, Rule 10) *"Tob shebe goyyim harog"* ("Even the best of the Gentiles should all be killed'). Whether or not the Zohar is a late or an early work, it contains all of the critical concepts of the Kabbalah, wound throughout a fantastic commentary on the Books of Moses (the Pentateuch), reinterpreting them to teach an emanationist system of divinity (which includes the diabolical), stemming from the primordial man Adam Kadmon, split into two pillars of male and female, which must be reintegrated and balanced, ritually, sexually and through the reconquest of Eretz Israel, the greater land of Israel. The spiritual lineage of occult Egypt is contained in the Zohar.

Zoroaster: (ca. 1000 B.C.) Founder of the Perso-Iranian dual-god religion. Zoroastrianism, which teaches a dualistic opposition between two gods, one good (Ormuzd or Ahura Mazda), the other evil (Ahriman or Angra Mainyu). Unlike Christianity, where evil is always a lack or deficiency—the devil having been created good and much weaker than his Creator, subsequently falling into the defects of evil)—the evil spirit in Zoroaster's religion is a powerful entity equal to God. The Zoroastrian conception of duality is paralleled in the kabbalistic concept of the Double Mind through the two pillars of the Tree of Life. Freemasonry for this reason occasionally references Zoroastrianism in its teachings.

Bibliography

Ahmed, Rollo. *The Black Art.* 1936.

Ali, Maulana Muhammad, trans. *The Holy Qur'an: Arabic Text with English Translation and Commentary.* Ohio: Ahmadiyya Anjuman Isha'at Islam Lahore, 2002.

Anger, Kenneth. *Hollywood Babylon.* New York: Dell, 1975.

Barruel, A. *Memoirs Illustrating the History of Jacobinism.* Trans. Robert Clifford.

Baum, L. Frank. *The Marvelous Land of Oz.* 1904.
Beta, Hymenaeus, ed., *The Equinox* 3, no. 10. York Beach: Samuel Weiser, 1990.

Bierce, Ambrose. *The Devil's Dictionary.* New York: Dover Publications, 1993.

Blavatsky, Helena, *The Secret Doctrine.*

Booth, Martin. *A Magick Life: A Biography of Aleister Crowley.* London: Hodder and Stoughton, 2000.

Brandon, Jim, (William N. Grimstad), *Rebirth of Pan,* Firebird Press, 1983.

Brandon, Jim, (William N. Grimstad), *Weird America* New York: E.P. Dutton, 1978.

Bowart, Walter, *Operation Mind Control,* 1978.

Burton, Richard Francis, *The Jew, the Gypsy and El Islam.* Kessinger Publishing, 2003.

Cabell, James Branch. *Jurgen: A Comedy of Justice.* Grosset & Dunlap, 1927.

Cahill, Rev. E. *Freemasonry and the Anti-Christian Movement.* Dublin: M. H. Gill and Son, 1952.

Carter, John. *Sex and Rockets: The Occult World of Jack Parsons.* Los Angeles: Feral House, 1999.

Chaucer, Geoffrey. *Troilus and Cressida and The Canterbury Tales.* London: William Benton, 1952.

Clarke, Arthur C. *Childhood's End.* New York: Ballantine

Books, 1974.

Clausen, Henry C. *Clausen's Commentaries on Morals and Dogma.* San Diego: The Supreme Council, 33°, Ancient and Accepted Scottish Rite of Freemasonry Southern Jurisdiction, U.S.A., 1974.

Clausen, Henry C. *Masons Who Helped Shape Our Nation.* San Diego: The Supreme Council, 33°, Ancient and Accepted Scottish Rite of Freemasonry, Southern Jurisdiction, U.S.A., 1976.

Cohen, Abraham. *Everyman's Talmud: The Major Teachings of the Rabbinic Sages.* Reprint. New York: Schocken Books, 1995.

Cohen, Samuel S. *B'nai B'rith Manual.* Cincinnati: n.p., 1926.

Compton, Piers. *The Broken Cross: The Hidden Hand in the Vatican.* Veritas Publishing Company, 1990.

Constantine, Alex. *Psychic Dictatorship in the U.S.A.* Los Angeles: Feral House, 1995.

Corydon, Bent and Hubbard Jr., L. Ron. *L. Ron Hubbard: Messiah or Madman?* Secaucus: Lyle Stuart, 1987.

Crowley, Aleister. *AHA! (Being Liber CCXLII)* Tempe: New Falcon, 1996.

Crowley, Aleister. *Amphora.* 1908. N.p.: First Impressions, 1993.

Crowley, Aleister. *Collected Works.* 1906. Reprint. Des Plaines: Yogi Publication Society, n.d.

Crowley, Aleister. *The Confessions of Aleister Crowley: An Autohagiography.* London: Arkana, 1989.

Crowley, Aleister. *Diary of a Drug Fiend.* 1922. Reprint. York Beach: Samuel Weiser, 1970.

Crowley, Aleister. *Eight Lectures on Yoga.* 1939. Reprint. Phoenix: New Falcon, 1991.

Crowley, Aleister. *The Equinox: The Official Organ of the AA / The Official Organ of the O.T.O. / The Review of Scientific Illuminism Vol. III No I.* 1919. Reprint. N. p.: Mandrake Press & Holmes, n.d.

Crowley, Aleister. *The Giant's Thumb.* 1915. Reprint. N.p.: First Impressions, 1992.

Crowley, Aleister. *The Heart of the Master & Other Papers.* Tempe: New Falcon, 1997.

Crowley, Aleister. *Konx Om Pax.* 1907. Reprint. Chicago: Teitan Press, 1990.

Crowley, Aleister. *The Law is for All: The Authorized Popular Commentary on Liber Al vel Legis sub figura CCXX The Book of the Law.* Tempe: New Falcon, 1996.

Crowley, Aleister. *The Revival of Magick and Other Essays.* Tempe: New Falcon, 1998.

Crowley, Aleister. *The Scrutinies of Simon Iff.* Chicago: Teitan Press, 1987.

Crowley, Aleister. *Why Jesus Wept.* 1904. Reprint. N.p.: First Impressions, 1993.

Crowley, Aleister, Mary Desti, and Leila Waddell. *Magick: Liber ABA Book Four Parts I-IV.* York Beach: Samuel Weiser, 1997.

Crowley, Aleister, Mary Desti, and Victor Neuburg. *The Vision & The Voice with Commentary And Other Papers.* York Beach: Samuel Weiser, 1998.

Daraul, Arkon. *Secret Societies: A History.* New York: MJF Books, 1989.

Deacon, Richard, *A History of British Secret Service.* London: Granada Publishing, 1982.

De Poncins, Vicomte Léon. *Freemasonry and the Vatican: A Struggle for Recognition.* Trans. Timothy Tindal-Robertson. Palmdale: Omni/Christian Book Club, 1968.

Decker, J. Edward, ed. *The Dark Side of Freemasonry.* Lafayette: Huntington House, 1994.

Dillon, Monsignor George F. *The War of Antichrist with the Church and Christian Civilization.* 1885. Reprinted as *Grand Orient Freemasonry Unmasked as the Secret Power Behind Communism.* Palmdale, CA: Christian Bookclub of America, 1999.

Downard, James Shelby. *Carnivals of Life and Death.* Coeur d'Alene, Idaho: Independent History & Research, 2000.

Downard, James Shelby and Hoffman II, Michael A., *King-Kill/33.* Coeur d'Alene, ID: Independent History & Research, 1998.

Drury, Nevill. *Dictionary of Mysticism and the Occult*. New York: Harper & Row, 1985.

Drury, Nevill. *The History of Magic in the Modern Age: A Quest For Personal Transformation*. 2000.

Duncan, Malcolm C. *Masonic Ritual and Monitor*. New York: David McKay, n.d.

Eusebius. *The History of the Church from Christ to Constantine*. Trans. G. A. Williamson. New York: Dorset Press, 1984.

Faÿ, Bernard. *Revolution and Freemasonry, 1680-1800*. Boston: Little, Brown, and Company, 1935.

Feder, Don. *A Jewish Conservative Looks at Pagan America*. Lafayette, IN: Huntington House, 1993.

Ferreira, Cornelia R. *The Feminist Agenda Within the Catholic Church*. Toronto: Life Ethics Centre, 1987.

Finkelstein, Norman G. *Image and Reality of the Israel-Palestine Conflict*. London: Verso, 2003.

Finney, Rev. Charles G. *The Character, Claims and Practical Working of Freemasonry*. 1869. Reprint. Tyler: JKI Publishing, 1998.

Fort, Charles. *The Complete Books of Charles Fort: The Book of the Damned / Lo! / Wild Talents / New Lands*. New York: Dover Publications, 1974.

Gilbert, Arthur. *The Vatican Council and the Jews*. Cleveland: The World Publishing Company, 1968.

Gilbert, R. A., ed. *The Magical Mason: Forgotten Hermetic Writings of William Wynn Westcott, Physician and Magus*. The Aquarian Press, 1983.

Godwin, Joscelyn, Christian Chanel, and John P. Deveney. *The Hermetic Brotherhood of Luxor: Initiatic and Historical Documents of an Order of Practical Occultism*. York Beach: Samuel Weiser, 1995.

Goethe, Johann Wolfgang von. *Faust*. Trans. George Madison Priest. London: William Benton, 1952.

Goodrick-Clarke, Nicholas. *The Occult Roots of Nazism: Secret Aryan Cults and Their Influence on Nazi Ideology*. Washington Square: New York University Press, 1992.

Grant, Kenneth. *Aleister Crowley and The Hidden God*. London: Skoob Books, 1992.

Grant, Kenneth. *Cults of the Shadow*. London: Skoob Books, 1994.

Grant, Kenneth. *The Magickal Revival*. London: Skoob Books, 1991.

Grant, Kenneth. *Nightside of Eden*. London: Skoob Books, 1994.

Gregor, A. James. *The Faces of Janus: Marxism and Fascism in the Twentieth Century*. New Haven: Yale University Press, 2000.

Greenfield, T. Allen. "The Frankist Ecstatics of the Eighteenth Century." in *Agape: The Official Organ of the U.S. Grand Lodge of Ordo Templi Orientis*, 1 Feb. 1998, 2-3.

Greenfield, T. Allen. *The Story of The Hermetic Brotherhood of Light*. Stockholm: Looking Glass Press, 1997.

Grusd, Edward E. *B'nai B'rith: The Story of a Covenant*. New York: Appleton-Century, 1966.

Guazzo, Francesco Maria. *Compendium Maleficarum*. Trans. Montague Summers. Mineola: Dover, 1988.

Haining, Peter, ed. *The Necromancers: The Best of Black Magic and Witchcraft*. London: Hodder and Stoughton, 1971.

Hall, Manly P. *The Lost Keys of Freemasonry*. The Philosophical Research Society, 1976.

Hall, Manly P. *The Secret Teachings of All Ages*. Los Angeles: The Philosophical Research Society, 1997.

Heinlein, Robert, *Stranger in a Strange Land*. Putnam Publishing, 1961.

Hoffman, Michael Anthony, *Masonic Assassination*. Rialto Books, 1978.

Hoffman II, Michael A., *Judaism's Strange Gods*. Coeur d'Alene, Idaho, Independent History and Research, 2000.

Hoffman II, Michael A. *Secret Societies and Psychological Warfare*. Coeur d'Alene, Idaho, Independent History and Research, 2001.

Horne, Alexander, *King Solomon's Temple in the Masonic Tradition*. The Aquarian Press, 1972.

Howard, Michael. *The Occult Conspiracy: Secret Societies — Their Influence and Power in World History*. Destiny, 1989.

Hsia, R. Po-chia. *The Myth of Ritual Murder: Jews and Magic in Reformation Germany*. New Haven: Yale University Press, 1988.

Hunter, C. Bruce. *Masonic Dictionary*. Richmond: Macoy Publishing, 1996.

Hunter, Reverend Father Christopher. "Catholics & The Republic" in *The Angelus: A Journal of Roman Catholic Tradition*, Feb. 1987, 4-8.

Hutchinsons, Roger. *Aleister Crowley: The Beast Demystified*. Edinburgh: Mainstream Publishing, 1999.

Huysman, J.K., *Là-bas, or Down There* (trans. by Keene Wallace), 1891.

Idel, Moseh. *Kabbalah: New Perspectives*. New Haven: Yale University Press, 1988.

Jacobs, Steven L. and Mark Weitzman. *Dismantling the Big Lie: The Protocols of the Elders of Zion*. Jersey City: KTAV Publishing House, 2003.

Jefferson, Thomas. *The Philosophy of Jesus of Nazareth Extracted From the Account of His Life and Doctrines as Given by Matthew, Mark, Luke & John: Being an Abridgment of the New Testament For the Use of the Indians Unembarrassed With Matters of Fact or Faith Beyond the Level of Their Comprehension*. 1804. Reprinted as *Thomas Jefferson's Abridgment of the Words of Jesus of Nazareth*. Charlottesville: Mark A. Beliles, 1993.

The Jewish Encyclopedia
http://www.jewishencyclopedia.com

Jouin, Monseigneur [Ernest],. *Papacy and Freemasonry*. 1930. Reprint. N. p.: Christian Book Club of America, n.d.

Kaplan, Aryeh. *The Real Messiah? A Jewish Response to Missionaries*. New York: National Conference of Synagogue Youth/Union of Orthodox Jewish Congregations of America, 1985.

Kaplan, Aryeh. *Sefer Yetzirah: The Book of Creation*. York Beach: Red Wheel/Weiser, 1997.

Keith, Jim, *Mind Control, World Control: The Encyclopedia of*

Mind Control. Adventures Unlimited Press, 1997.

"Killing for Satan." *Fortean Times,* May 2003, 16-18.

King, Francis, ed. *Crowley on Christ.* London: The C. W. Daniel Company, 1974.

King, Francis. *Mega Therion: The Magickal World of Aleister Crowley.* Creation Books, 2004.

King, Francis. *Modern Ritual Magic: The Rise of Western Occultism.* Dorset: Prism Press, 1989.

King, Francis, ed. *Ritual Magic of the Golden Dawn: Works by S. L. MacGregor Mathers and Others.* Destiny Books, 1997.

King, Francis, ed. *The Secret Rituals of the OTO.* New York: Samuel Weiser, 1973.

King, Francis. *Sexuality, Magic and Perversion.* Los Angeles: Feral House, 2002.

Knight, Stephen. *The Brotherhood: The Secret World of the Freemasons.* Acacia Press, 1985.

Knight, Stephen. *Jack the Ripper: The Final Solution.* Chicago: Academy Chicago Publishers, 1988.

Koestler, Arthur. *The Thirteenth Tribe.* New York: Random House, 1976.

Ko Hsüan (Aleister Crowley). *Tao Te Ching.* York Beach: Samuel Weiser, 1995.

König, Peter-R. "The Ordo Templi Orientis Phenomenon." English on-line version of *Das O.T.O. Phänomen.* http://homepage.sunrise.ch/homepage/prkoenig/phenomen.htm

Küntz, Darcy, ed. *The Golden Dawn Source Book.* Edmonds: Holmes Publishing, 1996.

LaVey, Anton Szandor. *The Satanic Bible.* New York: Avon Books, 1969.

Lazare, Bernard. *Antisemitism: Its History and Causes.* University of Nebraska Press, 1995.

Leadbeater, C.W., *Science of the Sacraments.* Kessinger Publishing, 1997.

Levi, Eliphas, *The Dogma and Ritual of High Magic.*

Levi, Eliphas. *Transcendental Magic: Its Doctrine and Ritual*. Trans. Arthur Edward Waite. 1896.

Machen, Arthur, *The Great God Pan*. 1894.

Mackey, Albert G. *The History of Freemasonry: Its Legendary Origins*. Gramercy Books, 1996.

Macoy, Robert. *A Dictionary of Freemasonry*. New York: Gramercy Books, 2000.

Mahl, Thomas E. *Desperate Deception: British Covert Operations in the United States, 1939-44*. Brassey's, 1999.

Mannix, Daniel P. *The Hellfire Club*. New York: ibooks, 2001.

Martinez, Mary Ball. *The Undermining of the Catholic Church*. Mexico: 1998.

Mathers, S. L. MacGregor, trans. *The Qabalah Unveiled*.

Matt, Daniel Chanan, *Zohar: The Book of Enlightenment*. New York: Paulist Press, 1983.

Maugham, W. Somerset, *The Magician*.

Metzger, Richard, ed. *Book of Lies: The Disinformation Guide to Magick and the Occult*. New York: The Disinformation Company, 2003.

Meyrink, Gustav. *The Golem*. Reprint. Dover Publications, 1986.

Millegan, Kris, ed. *Fleshing Out Skull & Bones: Investigations Into America's Most Powerful Secret Society*. Trine Day, 2003.

Miller, Edith Starr [Lady Queenborough]. *Occult Theocracy*. Los Angeles: The Christian Book Club of America.

Molnar, Thomas, *The Pagan Temptation*, Erdmans, 1987.

Molnar, Thomas, *Utopia, The Perennial Heresy*, Sheed and Ward, 1967.

Morgan, Capt. William. *Illustrations of Masonry by One of the Fraternity Who has devoted Thirty Years to the Subject*. 1827.

Newton, Michael. *Raising Hell: An Encyclopedia of Devil Worship and Satanic Crime*. New York: Avon Books, 1993.

Nietzsche, F. W. *The Antichrist*. Trans. H. L. Mencken. New York: Alfred A. Knopf, 1941.

Owen, Alex, *The Place of Enchantment: British Occultism and the Culture of the Modern*, University of Chicago Press, 2004.

Parfrey, Adam, ed. *Apocalypse Culture*. New York: Amok Press, 1987.

Parfrey, Adam, ed. *Apocalypse Culture*. Expanded and Revised Edition. Los Angeles: Feral House, 1990.

Parfrey, Adam, "Pederastic Park?" in *Answer Me!* (Volume Three), AK Press, 1994.

Pike, Albert. *Liturgy of the Ancient and Accepted Scottish Rite of Freemasonry for the Southern Jurisdiction of the United States.* Kessinger Publishing Company

Pike, Albert. *Morals and Dogma of the Ancient and Accepted Scottish Rite of Freemasonry*. Roberts Publishing, 1966.

Pope John Paul II. *Spiritual Pilgrimage: Texts on Jews and Judaism 1979-1995*. Ed. Eugene J. Fisher and Leon Klenicki. New York: Crossroad, 1995.

Preuss, Arthur. *A Study in American Freemasonry*. St. Louis, MO: B. Herder, 1908.

The Proceedings of the United States Anti-Masonic Convention: Held in Philadelphia, September 11, 1830. Embracing the Journal of the Proceedings, the Reports and the Address to the People. Republished. Montague: Acacia Press, 1996. http://www.crocker.com/~acacia/text_usamc.html

Quinn, D. Michael. *Early Mormonism and the Magic World View*. Salt Lake City: Signature Books, 1998.

Rabelais, Francois. *Gargantua and Pantagruel*. Trans. Sir Thomas Urquhart and Peter Motteux. London: William Benton, 1952.

Rager, Rev. Fr. John Clement. *The Political Philosophy of St. Robert Bellarmine*. Spokane: Apostolate of Our Lady of Siluva, 1995.

Ratzinger, Joseph Cardinal. *Many Religions—One Covenant: Israel, the Church and the World*. Trans. Graham Harrison. San Francisco: Ignatius Press, 1999.

Ratzinger, Joseph Cardinal. *Salt of the Earth: Christianity and the Catholic Church at the End of the Millennium*. Trans. Adrian Walker. San Francisco: Ignatius Press, 1997.

Regardie, Israel, ed. *777 and Other Qabalistic Writings of Aleister Crowley Including Gematria & Sephir Sephiroth.* York Beach: Samuel Weiser, 1977.

Regardie, Israel. *The Eye in the Triangle.* Phoenix: Falcon, 1982.

Regardie, Israel, ed. *Gems From The Equinox: Instructions by Aleister Crowley for His Own Magickal Order.* Phoenix: Falcon, 1986.

Regardie, Israel. *The Golden Dawn: An Account of the Teachings, Rites and Ceremonies of the Order of the Golden Dawn.* St. Paul, MN: Llewellyn, 1984.

Regardie, Israel. *The Tree of Life: A Study in Magic.* York Beach: Samuel Weiser, 1972.

Reisman, Judith A. *Kinsey: Crimes & Consequences.* The Institute for Media Education, 2000.

Reuss, Theodor and Crowley, Aleister. *O.T.O. Rituals and Sex Magick.* I-H-O Books, 1999.

Robbins, Alexandra, "Powerful Secrets." *Vanity Fair,* July 2004, 116-21, 156-58.

Robbins, Alexandra. *Secrets of the Tomb: Skull and Bones, The Ivy League, and the Hidden Paths of Power.* Boston: Little, Brown and Company, 2002.

Roberts, Rev. Alexander, and Donaldson, James, eds. *The Ante-Nicene Fathers, Vol. I: The Apostolic Fathers/Justin Martyr/Irenaeus.* Grand Rapids: Wm. B. Eerdmans, 1989.

Robinson, John, *A Pilgrim's Path: Freemasonry and the Religious Right,* M. Evans & Co., 1993.

Robinson, John J. *Born in Blood: The Lost Secrets of Freemasonry.* New York: M. Evans & Company, 1989.

Rosenberg, Elliot. *But Were They Good for the Jews? Over 150 Historical Figures Viewed From a Jewish Perspective.* Secaucus: Birch Lane Press, 1997.

Samberg, Joel. *The Jewish Book of Lists.* Secaucus: Citadel Press, 1998.

Savedow, Steve, trans. *Sepher Rezial Hemelach: The Book of the Angel Rezial.* York Beach: Red Wheel/Weiser, 2000.
Scholem, Gershom. *Kabbalah.* New York: Meridian, 1978.

Scholem, Gershom. *On the Kabbalah and Its Symbolism*. New York: Schocken Books, 1974.

Scholem, Gershom, ed. *Zohar: The Book of Splendor*. New York: Schocken Books, 1977.

Secret Ritual of the Thirty-third and Last Degree: Sovereign Grand Inspector General of the Ancient and Accepted Scottish Rite of Freemasonry. Kessinger Publishing Company.

Secret Societies Illustrated: Comprising the So-Called Secrets of Freemasonry, Adoptive Masonry, Oddfellowship, Good Templarism, Temple of Honor, United Sons of Industry, Knights of Pythias and the Grange. 1879. Reprint. Chicago: Ezra A. Cook.

Seligmann, Kurt. *The History of Magic and the Occult*. New York: Gramercy Books, 1997.

Shahak, Israel. *Jewish History, Jewish Religion*. London, England: Pluto Press.

Short, Martin, *Inside the Brotherhood*, Dorset Press, 1990.

Silbiger, Steven. *The Jewish Phenomenon: Seven Keys to the Enduring Wealth of a People*. Atlanta: Longstreet Press, 2000.

Smith, Timothy d'Arch. *The Books of the Beast: Essays on Aleister Crowley, Montague Summers, Francis Barret and Others*. Crucible, 1987.

Smith, Wolfgang. *Teilhardism and the New Religion: A Thorough Analysis of the Teachings of Pierre Teilhard de Chardin*. Rockford, IL: Tan Books, 1988.

Steichen, Donna. *Ungodly Rage: The Hidden Face of Catholic Feminism*. San Francisco: Ignatius Press, 1992.

Steinsaltz, Adin. *The Essential Talmud*. Northvale: Jason Aronson, 1992.

Steinsaltz, Rabbi Adin. *Opening the Tanya: Discovering the Moral & Mystical Teachings of a Classic Work of Kabbalah*. San Francisco: Jossey-Bass, 2003.

Steinsaltz, Rabbi Adin. *The Talmud: The Steinsaltz Edition/A Reference Guide*. New York: Random House, 1989.

Steinsaltz, Rabbi Adin. *The Talmud: The Steinsaltz Edition*. New York: Random House, 1997-2002.

Summers, Montague. *The History of Witchcraft.* New York: Barnes & Noble, 1993.

Summers, Montague. *Witchcraft and Black Magic.* Mineola: Dover Publications, 2000.

Suster, Gerald. *The Legacy of the Beast: The Life, Work and Influence of Aleister Crowley.* York Beach: Samuel Weiser, 1990.

Sutin, Lawrence. *Do What Thou Wilt: A Life of Aleister Crowley.* New York: St. Martin's Press, 2000.

Sutton, Anthony. *America's Secret Establishment: An Introduction to the Order of Skull & Bones.* Waterville: Trine Day, 2002.

Symonds, John. *The Great Beast: The Life and Magick of Aleister Crowley.* Frogmore: Mayflower Books, 1973.

Taxil, Leo [Gabriel Jogand-Pagés]. *Masonry Exposed and Explained.* St. Louis: Church Progress, 1891.

Temple, Robert K.G., *The Sirius Mystery,* Sidgwick and Jackson, 1976.

Valiente, Doreen. *The Rebirth of Witchcraft.* Phoenix Publishing, 1989.

Vennari, John. *Close-ups of the Charismatic Movement.* Los Angeles: Tradition in Action, 2002.

Vennari, John, *The Permanent Instruction of the Alta Vendita.* Tan Books, 1999.

Von Hildebrand, Dietrich. *Trojan Horse in the City of God,* Sophia Institute Press, 1993.

Waite, Arthur Edward, *Book of Black Magic and Pacts.*

Waite, Arthur Edward, *The Holy Kabbalah: A Mystical Interpretation of the Scriptures.* New York: Citadel Press, 1995.

Waite, Arthur Edward. *A New Encyclopaedia of Freemasonry.* New York: Wings Books, 1996.

Walker, Benjamin. *Tantrism: Its Secret Principles and Practices.* The Aquarian Press, 1982.

Washington, Peter, *Madame Blavatsky's Baboon.* Schocken, 1996.

Wasserman, James, *The Slaves Shall Serve,* Sekmet Books, 2004.

Wasserman, James. *The Templars and the Assassins: The Militia of Heaven.* Inner Traditions, 2001.

Webster, Nesta H. *Secret Societies and Subversive Movements.* Palmdale: Omni Publications.

Wiener, Norbert. *God & Golem, Inc.: A Comment on Certain Points where Cybernetics Impinges on Religion.* Cambridge: The M.I.T. Press, 1964.

Wiesel, Elie. *The Golem: The Story of a Legend.* New York: Summit Books, 1983.

Williamson, Jack, *Darker Than You Think.* Fantasy Press, 1948.

Wilmshurst, W. L. *The Meaning of Masonry.* New York: Gramercy Books, 1980.

Wilson, Colin. *The Occult: A History.* New York: Random House, 1971.

Wilson, Robert Anton. *Cosmic Trigger: The Final Secret of the Illuminati.* New York: Pocket Books, 1978.

Wilson, Robert Anton. *Everything Is Under Control: Conspiracies, Cults, and Cover-Ups.* New York: Harper Perennial, 1998.

Wise, David and Ross, Thomas B. *The Invisible Government.* New York: Bantam, 1965.

Yarker, John. *The Secret High Degree Rituals of the Masonic Rite of Memphis.* Kessinger.

Yates, Frances A. *The Rosicrucian Enlightenment.* London: Routledge, 2000.